Laughin'fertility

A Bundle of Observations for the Baby-Making Challenged

Lisa Safran

KOKO Press, Inc.

Published by
KOKO Press, Inc.

ISBN 0-9669858-1-8

Cover design and art by Tabitha Pearson Marshall

Printed in the U.S.A.

This book is dedicated to the little baby
I imagine in my mind's eye.
A precious angel who is hiding until the time is right.
He or she is, and always will be,
my baby.

Note To the Reader

The intention of this book is not to provide you with
sound medical facts and advice on treatments associated
with infertility but rather, with wildly wacky
observations that will surely keep you smiling throughout
your baby journey. . . .

. . . because sometimes it's better to laugh than to cry.

Spit Happens:
An Introduction

Some couples just look at each other funny and voilà they make a baby. Others, like you and me, are struggling.

And boy, can it be trying at times.

It's a test of our strength. The strength of our relationship. It's a financial strain. A strain on our mattress springs. This is serious business.

But hey, spit happens.

If you're reading this book, all I can say is that I'm sorry.

Sorry that conception isn't coming to you and your partner so easily. I know how it feels. My husband and I have been riding the kiddy ride for nearly five years.

But if you are reading this book, I am also very happy for you. Happy that you are seeking humor to cope with your situation. (And only you know how ridiculously amusing the situation can be at times.)

As in many trying moments in our lives, humor often softens the blow. In fact, laughter can help you to keep a positive attitude, reduce stress and avoid beating the heck out of each other.

While you read through this book, you'll discover situations, procedures, emotions and overall observations you may have already experienced—or are about to face.

But this book is not here to inform you of the technical aspects of infertility. (OK, I finally said the dreaded "I" word.) You won't find a ton of facts, case studies or footnotes on every other page citing a reputable source of information. The doctors, along with the stack of serious reference books you've already purchased, will take care of that end.

This infertility book is different. It's here to point out the lighter side of what is an already heavy situation. Written by someone who has already been there, done that, cried hard, laughed hard—all to make a baby. Why did I write this book? Well, my intention is to point out a bundle of funny observations associated with the treatment of infertility in hopes of helping you maintain a positive perspective as you embark on your own baby journey.

For years my husband and I used birth control. The thought of getting pregnant! But later on in our marriage, when we finally got serious about making a baby, we realized there was a glitch. All those years of caution, months and months of refills on my pill prescription, all that time, money and lambskin, so much effort down the tubes, and I'm not talking fallopian.

I even remember one month early on in our marriage when my period was considerably late. We were terrified I was pregnant. As time passed, we were terrified we'd never be pregnant.

It took years, an entire process, for our perspective to change. I guess it all boiled down to readiness. At the time we were practicing birth control methods neither one of us was ready for a baby. Our careers were booming, vacation plans were spur of the moment and sex happened anywhere, anytime we wanted. (Well, not really, but it sounds good.) A baby wouldn't have made sense then.

Once we were ready for a little addition to our family, we stopped using birth control. We were carefree, uncomplicated, spontaneous. For the first six to seven months, we happily fooled around, anticipating the making of one of us. But as the months rolled by, and the novelty of regular, unprotected sex wore off, we began to worry.

All of our friends who had already conceived said to give it a year. That was approximately the time we would need for conception to occur. So, for a few more months we continued "casual" sex, but quite honestly, neither of us was having that much fun anymore. Deep down, we both feared there was something wrong.

To take control of our impending situation, we began a more methodical approach to our efforts. Each month, we timed our sexual activities around my ovulation hoping for optimal conditions. If my period was a minute late, we thought, "Maybe this is the month!"

No such luck. Each month, my reliable "friend" showed up. I was beginning to hate the sight of her crimson face.

For the next few months, our concerns grew but neither of us talked about it much. In denial of an issue bigger than perhaps we wanted to face, we continued to monitor my ovulation, avoid verbalizing our fears and hope for a miracle.

Those few months slipped into years. We managed to sprinkle in lots of distractions, helping time to fly by. More vacations, bigger projects at the office, but still something was missing. After about two years of exhausting, wishful thinking—and no reproduction whatsoever—we mustered up the courage to finally start talking about our situation and see a "specialist."

The kiddy ride, a bumpy one at that, was about to begin.

We purchased two tickets for the ride. One for me at the ob-gyn. One for my husband at the Semen Analysis Laboratory. (Notice how I capitalize the letters. Like it's the White House or some other important place.)

After extensive blood work and a pregnancy test (was my doctor trying to be cruel?), I passed the initial inspection. My hormone levels were OK, my other counts were fine and no, I wasn't pregnant.

Upon completion of my husband's first semen analysis, we waited. And waited. Until the phone rang. It was my ob-gyn.

Our minds were racing with "what ifs." I seemed to have a clean bill of health. Did that mean there was something wrong with hubby?

On the one hand, we wanted to hear "yes." It would have meant knowing what the problem was and being able to start dealing with it.

On the other hand, we wanted to hear "no." Then we could go back to pretending there was nothing wrong and keep trying until we were well into our fifties.

On the third hand (hey, when you're stressed you can have as many hands as you need), we were both waiting for the other person to pick up the phone.

"Abnormal," my ob-gyn said into my ear.

I sat back on the sofa and closed my eyes as she babbled on about what sounded like morphing, varicose veins and something about the speed at which his "little guys" were moving. I barely understood what she was saying but I got enough to know that we were boarding the kiddy cart. The amusement park attendant was strapping on our seatbelts. I took a deep breath in anticipation of the excitement—and of the ride we were about to endure.

At first, there was nothing funny about our situation. In fact, I lost my sense of humor completely. All I did was cry. Cry and exercise excessively, sometimes simultaneously, for months.

We scheduled an appointment with our first specialist: a urologist. He would examine my husband's "situation."

While we waited the two months to see him, we bought every fertility and infertility book under the sun. We tried every "trick" passed on through books, magazine articles and people with large families.

Like raising my hips up on a stack of pillows. Or holding my labia shut after lovemaking to keep the sperm from spilling out. Herbal teas. Chinese roots. Cough syrup moments before doing "it" to make my cervical fluid stringier and more conducive to helping the sperm travel toward my ovaries. Lovemaking every day. Lovemaking every third day. Holding my legs up in the air for twenty minutes after the actual act of, hoping that gravity would kick in.

By the day we were scheduled to see the doctor, my flexibility had increased, my cough was gone, but no, we weren't pregnant.

That specialist recommended us to *another* specialist who in turn referred us to specialists closer to our home. We spent a great deal of time going from specialist to specialist, looking for causes and solutions. Before we knew it, after a few unsuccessful stabs at IUI (intrauterine insemination), we were enrolled in an IVF program (in vitro fertilization) at a hospital nearby.

Unfortunately, a few months later, we relocated to another state for a career opportunity. We were either going to travel over two bridges every day for blood work, sonograms and an egg retrieval, or transfer our "IVF-forts" to a new hospital.

All those months of waiting, procrastinating, investigating and searching had added up to years. And now, with our relocation, we had to take a few giant steps backwards. It was fate, I kept telling myself to keep from falling apart. Our new hospital would bring us a baby.

Somewhere along the way, as we got deeper and deeper into the baby-making process, I began to see the humor in our position. Call it a defense mechanism but it worked. We started finding humor in almost every situation: the doctors' appointments, my pelvic exams, our decision to go boxer over jockey shorts. Looking back, I'm sure if we didn't laugh so much, we would have cried a lot more.

In time, I realized our problem was merely a challenge. I was not going to be beaten by our situation. And I knew that I could laugh at a challenge because challenges can be conquered. We believe, and always will, that anything good in this life, really good, is worth working for—and laughing about. It made perfect sense then. And, now, it makes sense all over again.

For years, I have been writing this book in my head, my heart and my funnybone. With every doctor's visit, every blood test, every shot of hormones, I observed myself and my husband going through the grueling challenge and thinking "This is nuts!" I had to laugh. Reminding myself to find the funny side has helped me to get the right perspective while reaching for our ultimate goal: a baby.

In fact, I believed in all of our hard work so much that I self-published this book. It was a personal and financial investment, a rather scary one at that, but so was my baby-making challenge. And I survived it, I believe, only because of a perspective laced with laughter.

Of course, a major thanks goes out to my husband. If his sperm wasn't imperfect, I wouldn't be going through a process that is hopefully going to make the baby that I know is so destined for this world. Plus, none of us would be reading this book.

Now for the big question—did we finally have our baby? At the time of writing this introduction I had no idea. In fact, this entire book was written before any final results came in. In fact, we were just beginning an IVF cycle. Our baby couldn't have been born until at least the spring of 1999.

By now, as you read this book, our baby should either be on the verge of being born, already born, or not coming at all.

It doesn't matter right now what our results were because I want you to learn to laugh at the process in order to distract you from worrying about the outcome. Yes, think baby. Think happy baby thoughts. But think laughter. Lighten up. Get through your baby-making challenge with a smile on your face.

And when your baby-making challenge is complete and your sides are splitting with laughter, you may find yourself blessed with the next highly amusing challenge: parenthood.

SECTION 1: FIRST STEPS

Background, Statistics and Other Thoughts to Teethe On

Baby-making Statistics

Over 6 million people are experiencing infertility every year.

Approximately 1 out of every 10 couples who are trying to conceive are having trouble.

Male and female issues are equally to blame for infertility woes.

There's 1 important thing to remember . . .

laugh when you can!

Enough to Make You Ga-ga

Everyone knows someone who is having trouble making a baby. A friend, a relative, a co-worker, doctor, lawyer, baker, candlestick maker. We're all over the place!

In the old days, no one knew anyone who had trouble making a baby. In fact, the people who had trouble making a baby didn't even realize that they, themselves, were the people having trouble making a baby.

When did things start to go so terribly wrong?

I'm glad you asked.

There are lots of theories—medical, environmental, genetic, cultural, underwearical. But there is little concrete evidence, few hard facts, why problems associated with fertility are on the rise. Many of us know we have a problem and we may know what that problem is. We just can't figure out why. Why, why, why?

To solve your common "why us?" dilemma (don't worry, you're not whining, you're normal), I've boiled down the infertility issue to three simple blame factors: bad air, nice clothes and parents.

We've all heard the bad air theories: too many toxins, not enough ozone, clumps of pesticides, the Mexican food you ate last night. Even with all our recycling and car pooling, anti-bacterials and sunblocks, fertility problems are worse than ever.

It's the air we're breathing. Plain and simple. And because air is so thin and it just slips through your fingers, none of us can get a handle on why, why, why.

Then there's the problem of nice clothes. Armani suits, designer jeans, Gucci bags, dry-clean-only sweaters, platinum-toe socks. Our closets are bursting! But boy, do we look good.

5

I blame clothes and the entire fashion industry for our baby-making problems. More and more of us can afford these fine clothes because we're working harder on the job, therefore earning more money (hopefully!). Longer hours. Weekends. Our thirties, forties. Oops. Forgot to schedule in baby-making. Honey, how are you for this Tuesday? Say around 10:30 in the morning? Yes, there will be an agenda. No, there won't be anyone taking minutes.

We're working vigorously and waiting until later in life before we stop for a moment to catch our breath, quit shopping and consider babies. I hate to bring up that darn clock but it truly is ticking. If only it were a Rolex.

The third most prevalent reason, and this one is a no-brainer, is our parents. Sorry, Mom and Dad, but the gene pool is a reality we're all swimming in. And now we're dying to procreate so that we can pass off the same lousy genes to our beloved little tikes. Then they'll be wading in the same pool years from now.

But I'm not here to put a damper on things. May I remind you of some of the other statistics—the good ones that prove couples like us have a really good chance of conceiving, despite our challenges.

In fact, your chances of becoming pregnant are higher in a reproductive program than the chances of an average couple in their own bedroom. Before we know it, no one will conceive the old-fashioned way. Whether we'll physically need to or because it's trés chic, we'll all utilize technology to procreate. By the year 3000 or so, we'll each have a pair of bronzed petri dishes on the mantel.

My point here—maybe it doesn't really matter why, why, why you were chosen to deal with this situation. The real issue is what, what, what. What are you two going to do about it? Hmmm? Perhaps you already know and you're actively involved in the process. Good for you! If you're getting ready to embark on a journey, then keep in mind that the statistics are changing all the time—and many of them keep changing for the better.

If you don't get freaked out, say nine out of ten times, by all the baby thoughts presently running through your brains, consider yourself ready to explore technology.

First Words:
Fertility, Infertility

From the moment I was awakened to the word "infertility," I realized there was another word in the wings, just waiting to be incorporated into my vocabulary: fertility.

You may first notice these two diabolically different words at the local bookstore. Gaze at the stacked shelves, take note of the titles of many of the books written for people like us and you'll see these two opposite words being used for basically the same topic. Interchangeable words, yet one sounds so much better than the other.

The bookstore may have categorized the section as "infertility," just as the world seems to, but there are quite a few authors out there who are looking at the situation with a more positive slant.

I myself purchased an "infertility book" (that was practically the title) and it covered all the different scenarios a couple could encounter. On that same day, I purchased a "fertility book," which claimed to be a complete guide to everything about our predicament. Barring writing style and unique case studies, content was pretty much the same in both books except one title took a 180-degree turn.

You may notice these two different words again when you start thinking about your first appointment with a specialist. Are you going to an infertility clinic or a fertility group? Are you being treated for infertility or fertility? Our society keeps going back and forth with this little word match. We're so confused.

Infertility. Fertility. Glass half empty. Glass half full. Negative. Positive. Problem. Solution. Which one is it?

At the present moment, you may be dealing with aspects of infertility but your goal is to be as fertile as a class of hormonally-crazed teenagers. The bookstore may feature an "infertility" shelf but you're not seeking advice on infertility. Just like a diet book—is anyone out there calling them "fat thighs and big butt" books? Set your sights on the solution, not the problem, and you're sure to survive.

So my advice to you is to clear things up from the get-go by focusing on the positive—your goal. For starters, try saying "I am dealing with issues of *fertility*. I am seeking the guidance of a *fertility* specialist. My goal is to be as *fertile* as those teenagers."

Technically, neither word—fertility or infertility—is a wrong choice; it's just your perspective that counts.

But if you still find yourself struggling with these two opposing words that can mean the same thing, then how about using a new word altogether?

The Birth of a Politically Correct Term for Infertility: Baby-making Challenged

Infertility. The word has become quite popular as couples everywhere cope with its many issues.

The couple from Iowa and their incredible septuplets. Headline news on the latest infertility drugs. New procedures, new successes, new controversies. Infertility—it's the latest trend.

Infertility. It has that "ility" sound that gives it a fighting chance of being positive. Ability. Stability. Virility. Tranquillity. Oh, how good it could be.

But then there's that little "in" stuck on the front end, setting the stage for a rather lousy day. Inability. Instability. Invirility. Intranquillity.

Upon consulting with a renowned word expert, Webster, I discovered the technical definition of infertility: an adjective, meaning not fertile, not productive, barren.

Ick.

How much more dismal could you get? Even if the definition fits your present situation, that doesn't mean we have to call it something so severe, so painful, so ick.

So gather 'round, Mr. Webster, Dr. Specialist and all you follicles in the making. It's time to get the word *in*fertility *out* of your vocabulary!

Let's get politically correct with the birth a new term for infertility: *Baby-making challenged.*

Your sperm cells deserve a swimming chance. Your eggs need not be scrambled in negativity. A more positive, "pc" term couldn't hurt the process one bit.

9

Being baby-making challenged merely means you've hit a bump in the road. A situation that makes it harder to make a baby. But good things—especially those that arrive in small, cuddly packages with soft skin and that smell really, really good—come to those who persevere with positivity, humility and laugh-ability.

QUIZ #1

Do You Want a Baby So Much that You're Willing to Take the Challenge?

Take this simple quiz to determine your readiness for the baby-making challenge:

1. What do you do when you see a baby?
a) make sappy smiley faces at him
b) look at your mate lovingly
c) get that warm and fuzzy feeling
d) cry
e) all of the above

2. The "challenge" makes you think of:
a) how tough the next few months, maybe years, will be
b) the chance that you could have your baby
c) Pepsi
d) practically nothing funny
e) all of the above

3. The extra bedroom in your house:
a) is basically empty
b) would look great in pastel blue or pink
c) is within an earshot of your bedroom
d) is secretly referred to by both of you as the nursery
e) all of the above

4. Lately, most of your reading has been:
a) books on fertility
b) the free pamphlets from the doctor's office
c) *Parents* magazine
d) your friend's copy of *What to Expect When You're Expecting*
e) all of the above

5. When the going gets tough, you and your mate get:
a) going
b) into a fight
c) out your favorite videos
d) hysterical with laughter
e) all of the above (except "a," of course)

QUIZ #2

Do You Have a Good Enough Sense of Humor to Get Through the Challenge?

Take this simple quiz to determine your humor level:

1. Why did you buy this book?
   a) it sounded different
   b) it seemed unusually light-hearted
   c) it was recommended
   d) I'm desperate
   (e) all of the above

2. Your own laugh sounds something like a:
   a) tiny giggle
   b) pig snort
   c) wheeze
   d) truck backing up
   (e) a combination of all of the above

3. You laugh at the following (please check all that apply):
   [X] clowns
   [X] comedians/politicians
   [X] the preposterous
   [X] the ridiculous
   [X] the extreme
   [ ] natural body odors
   [X] farts (and the fact that it's listed here as one of your choices)
   [X] dirty jokes
   [X] wacky situations
   [ ] uncomfortable positions
   [ ] your predicament
   [X] your mate
   [X] yourself
   [ ] other_____

Congratulations!

You passed both quizzes!

All of your answers were correct.

Your intelligence, honesty
and sense of humor
have prepared you for the
baby-making challenge.

Consider yourself ready to continue . . .

CRIB SHEET:

How to Respond to Friends and Family Who Say Really Insensitive Things

"When are you kids going to have kids already?"

This one usually comes from the loudmouth aunt you don't see all that often. You bump into her at a cousin's wedding and, after a preliminary hug, kiss and idle chitchat, she stares deeply at the two of you. Realizing you've been together for quite some time (the last time you saw her was *your* wedding), she gets that concerned wrinkle in her brow and asks the dreaded question.

"Soooo?"

Sew buttons, you recite in your head.

"Soooo, when are you two going to have a baby?"

At this point, he looks at you, you look at him and, depending upon whose aunt she is, someone mutters a response.

Don't panic, you can go a few different ways with your answer.

The polite route would be to say "Oh, we're working on it, Aunt Busy Bee." Smile and hush up. This leaves your aunt wondering—are they pregnant already? Are they trying this month? Either way, your answer is enough to keep her satisfied until the next family affair.

However, if you're hormonal and feeling really uncomfortable in your crunchy taffeta dress, you can lay it on but good.

"Glad you asked, Aunt Rumor-monger. I've been needing to talk to someone for weeks about our little problem." At this point, escort her to an empty table by the kitchen. Give her every gory detail you can think of—sperm counts, pelvic exams, the ampules of hormone-stimulating drugs you've got in that cute little beaded purse. If she hasn't passed out by the time you're through, then guaranteed, she's lost her appetite before the Viennese table ever arrives.

"Who's the problem?"

Don't you hate this one? Why does it even matter? Why are we always looking to put the blame on someone? What a society we live in. Would people ask this question if you had to foreclose on your house? Or if the toilet backed up? Would people need to know who caused the problem then?

People just want to know. They need to know. It makes their day so much more complete. And, deep down, there's a side of you that wants to clear your own name of the blame. C'mon admit it. Nobody likes a troublemaker.

Think back to your childhood. Lots of fingerpointing. He did it, she did it. They started it, not me. Life was much easier when we could free ourselves by exposing others. It's like when you and your brother were playing ball in the house—until the ball crashed into the table and shattered that crystal thing Mom called her favorite vase in the whole world.

On the one hand, you wanted to blurt out, "He did it! It's his fault! Not me. I'm clean!" It would have gotten you off the hook completely. Mom wouldn't have thought badly of you. Just your dopey brother.

But at the same time you knew you were both dribbling that basketball in the living room. You were in it together. Therefore you probably said nothing and were sent to your rooms.

When friends and family ask you who the problem is, tell them this: the baby.

She's the problem. *She's* shy. Or *he's* just not ready to enter into this cruel world yet where people ask dumb questions. Say it with a smile and the askers are sure to back off without feeling slighted.

That type of answer will make you both feel like team players. Plus, you'll relish in watching friends and family continuing to burst with curiosity.

"You two just need to relax a little."

Statistics say that if you haven't conceived naturally in about one year's time, then you should consider seeking the advice of a fertility specialist. If, like many other couples, you've been trying for years—and I'm talking multiple birthdays that have passed you by, a myriad of Thanksgivings that have been carved away, a slew of Labor Day weekends that have been spent fighting traffic—then I doubt very much that relaxation is the issue here. Sure you've had tense moments but you haven't been stressed out all this time. It's a vicious cycle, though; the longer you can't conceive, the more stressed you may be growing.

But despite the normal up-and-down moments in any person's life, people will continue to insist that you both just need to stop thinking about baby-making in order to succeed. They'll swear that all you need is to spend a long weekend away at some bed-and-breakfast. Or just take a few long drives to the beach, mountains or green pastures. Somehow people think, despite your years of struggle and your present enrollment in a fertility program, that a dose of R&R will be your cure-all.

Why do some people keep this up even after they know you're going through what you're going through? Don't they get it? Here's a theory: *they* can't face what you're coping with. *They* can't imagine that there is actually a situation here that needs more than just a simple day by the pool. I guess *they* can't handle it.

You might try telling them that you have never been more relaxed in your life. In fact, if you were any more relaxed you'd be comatose. But the fact that they remain in this type of denial is really beginning to stress you out.

"Do you realize you could have two, three, even four babies?"

This question usually comes from the friends and family who've been watching way too much TV and reading too many supermarket tabloids.

Yes, there is a chance of multiple births with many of today's fertility treatments. I know that. You know that. And, yes, we've all heard about the family who gave birth to seven. But so what!

If you're moving forward on the fertility path, then you have an inkling of the multiple issue. And you may have already decided, like my husband and I did, it's all (or at least some) or nothing.

Smart answer to this insensitive question: "Well, then, do you realize you're going to have to buy two, three, even four gifts every birthday and holiday? And none of those group gifts. Everyone in our litter gets their own special present for every single occasion. I suggest you start saving now."

"Are you sure you want to do this?"

Maybe you should ask them these questions before you give your answer: "Are you sure you want to give a speech to 8,000 people on a subject you know very little about? Are you sure you want to drive down that dark road not knowing if it leads to your destination? Are you sure you want to marry that no-good, jobless, toothless man who belches in public?" How can we be sure about making any scary decision?

You know you want the end product—a baby. You're just not sure of all the stuff you need to do to get to that point. Who would be?

But if it's the only path you can take to get to the end point, then what the heck. You're not sure you want to do *this* but clearly you know you want *that*. If you tell people that thought, in just those precise and convoluted words, they'll be too confused to ask another question.

"I know a woman at work who is going through the exact same thing."

Why do people think this statement is comforting? To a baby-making challenged couple, these words sound like pity, small talk or just plain gossip.

We don't care if you know other people in our predicament. It doesn't matter that millions of people are dealing with the same issues. We're concerned about our own right now, thank you very much.

At the same time, the friend or family member who makes this statement to you is then sharing that same thought with the poor woman at work (you know, the one who is going through the exact

Laughin'fertility

same thing you are) in hopes of comforting her too. You'd think this friend is a matchmaker, setting people up based on shared hobbies or medical problems.

What to say to this statement: "Do I know this woman? [long pause, for effect] In fact, do *you* know this woman?"

"What you're going through isn't that bad. At least you have options."

Obviously, this statement comes from those who aren't going through what you two are. First off, what you're going through *is* that bad. It's horrible, emotionally draining and completely unfair—let's get that straight from the beginning.

The problem with the above statement is that it comes from those who haven't experienced the struggles of baby-making challenges. In our situation—actually, any situation, for that matter—misery loves company and respects it too. If another baby-making challenged couple made this comment, you probably wouldn't get your back up. It would be OK, perhaps even a wise thing to say. But if you haven't walked our rocky path, then zip it.

Therefore, deal with this comment like any sensible adult in your position would: get up on your soap box. "Options? Let me tell you about options in our cruel and crazy world . . . "

"I was afraid to tell you but I'm pregnant."

She's been a close friend for years and this is how she tells you her wonderful news? Before you write her off, let us see her side for a minute.

She's overjoyed with her pregnancy and wants to share the happiness with you. But on the flip side, she knows you've been trying for the same news for so long and the thought of laying this on you is devastating.

But by stating her news this way, she does nothing more than hurt you like never before. You're wounded that she feels compelled to sensor her conversations with you, particularly as they relate to babies. And, deep down, you're pissed that she's pregnant and you're not. What to do?

You love her but still, this might be a good time to be a bit catty, just for a minute or two. Tell her, "You know, these last five or six months, I've been thinking you were pregnant." (Lay it on thick). "You've put on so much weight and your ankles are puffy. Congratulations!" Then, when she looks at you with a blank stare, tell her you're just kidding, how this is such fantastic news, that you're happy for her, blah, blah, blah. You might want to give her a hug before she starts bawling.

"Are you pregnant yet?"

This question is the zinger. And if "shut-up" were a more socially acceptable saying in our world, I would suggest such a retort.

Once you've begun your baby-making challenge, your loved ones will be so concerned and excited for you that they'll be asking this question all too often. And, if you're like my nervous husband, even pondering this question in your own mind—at any stage in the process—is a jinx. Bad luck. Hurry, knock on wood.

Set the stage early on (perhaps on the same day you get the "sooo?" question from your nosy relatives) with this pre-question answer: "Please don't ask us if we're pregnant. We will tell you when there is good news to share."

If this doesn't work, dim the lights, draw the shades and disconnect all phone lines for what will hopefully become the first trimester.

A Warning

The following is not an insensitive question—it's more of an insensitive look.

If you've been experiencing the nonverbal stare—the one where people look at you with sad eyes and sorrowful brows—then beware. This usually comes from people you don't even know. Perhaps you'll come across these folk in a social setting where small children abound: a friend's baby's first birthday party, a neighbor's block party, the local swimming pool, the diner. As these strangers embrace their little ones, they'll give you that pathetic look, like they're thinking, "Oh, this poor couple obviously can't have kids or they would have by now."

The way to handle this uncomfortable stare is to stare right back. Then flip 'em the bird.

What Friends and Family _Can_ Say that Won't Send You Over the Edge

What to Say to a Baby-Making Challenged Couple: Helpful Guidelines for Friends and Family

Give your friends and family a copy of this page and tell them to practice these comforting lines. And remember, do not say more than two lines at once and, of course, no ad-libbing!

- I'm sorry
- I'm so sorry
- I'm really sorry
- I'm here for you guys if you need me in any way
- I still love you
- Oh man
- Are you OK?
- Wanna go out for lunch—my treat?
- Do you want to talk?
- Let me know how I can help you and when I should shut up.

Fill in your own helpful, non-irritating statements here:

I'm praying for you.
You're in my prayers

Share and Share Alike:
A Male/Female Approach

The difference between how men and women talk about their baby-making challenge with non-baby-making challenged men and women can be boiled down to this: the silent film versus the talking movie.

I don't mean to pull any of that Mars/Venus stuff, but men and women are different when it comes to talking about personal issues, particularly health-related ones. Perhaps this is stereotypical, but men are generally the nonverbal species. They don't want to talk about it, don't like to talk about it and, basically, don't know how to talk about it.

Whether it be a personal health problem or their deepest, darkest feelings, male conversation usually consists of silence, shoulder shrugs and a slap or two on the back.

In the gym locker room men might ask one another if they caught the game last night.

While actually watching the game last night, guys will talk about the game.

And any small talk during business meetings or by the water cooler usually focuses on the game and when they'll see each other at the gym next.

Where do you think "silent Tom" originated? There's an old legend about some guy named Tom who was baby-making challenged. He couldn't talk about his situation to anyone, barely his wife. So she dubbed him "silent Tom."

Ever hear of the "strong, silent" type? This little phrase developed through the years and for good reason. When has anyone referred to a man as the strong and highly verbal type? Strong and very communicative type? Strong and in-touch-with-his-feelings type? If poor Tom could have opened up, we'd be using the phrase "talkative Tom" a lot more.

Men have a hard enough time talking with their wives about menstrual cycles, swollen breasts and maxi pads each month. Now, throw in your baby-making challenge and many guys turn into mutes. In time, most learn how to open up to their spouses, but, when it comes to talking to friends, men just don't ask other men about babies. They either have them—or they don't. End of discussion that never started.

If male factor is the issue, then men are doubly dumb-founded. We're talking a test of manhood. (Well, the men aren't talking— it's just a figure of speech.) What guy would share his low sperm count with his buddies at the gym? Can you imagine tips on ejaculating into a sterile cup in between quarters at a basketball game? Sperm quality and quantity is a very touchy thing. It takes a real man to speak of it.

Women, on the other hand, usually can't keep quiet.

We're a different species, able to verbalize thoughts and emotions while barely moving our lips. We like to talk it through, talk it over, talk amongst ourselves, seek advice, receive acknowledgment, chew the fat, cover ground, share experiences, run it by and, basically, get it off our chests.

Step into the same gym where the men are down the hall shrugging and you'll find women starting their conversations in the locker room, continuing their chatter while peeing simultaneously in adjacent stalls and delving even deeper during step class. Women talk before business meetings and then continue with a follow-up meeting that usually requires lunch on Thursday. Yenta, blabbermouth, chatterbox, gossip—when have you ever heard these words describe a man?

Baby-making challenges are floodgates for female lips, allowing the information and experiences to flow freely. Women will form support groups, they'll share their experiences with strangers and they'll chew silent Tom's ear off with what-ifs and what-do-you-thinks.

Silent men, talking women and baby-making challenges—it's a phenomenon that has interested psychotherapists for years. But since most of them have been men, they've chosen not to talk about it.

A Visit With Grandpa: Explaining Your Situation to An Older Generation

My father-in-law is a wonderful 84-year-old man who has always taken an interest in our lives, even when he didn't have a clue as to what we were talking about.

One example that comes to mind is the day I explained my job as a freelance writer. It's a foreign profession to me sometimes, let alone a man who survived the Depression. When I told him that I was writing different types of advertisements he immediately assumed I was a jingle writer. Jingles were common in his day so they were something he could relate to. So, I write short little tunes that rhyme and sell soda at the same time.

When the Internet craze took over, he made some observations of his own. After talking about web sites (he calls them webbed sites), emails (these were messagings) and mousepads (mouse-traps), I could tell we were wedged in a generation gap.

Then came the day when my husband and I decided it was time to explain our baby-making challenge. All Dad knew was that his son had been married for over five years and no grandkids had been produced yet. I don't think the fertility issue popped up in his mind; in fact I'm sure it didn't—fertility is not part of his vocabulary. He probably was assuming we hadn't gotten around to babies yet so he respected our time frame and never asked. (Although he would drop subtle hints like reminding us that he was holding a special locket for when we have a little girl.)

Over dinner one night we explained our situation. As he passed the bread basket, I could tell by his empty stare that he was very confused. What happened to man and woman get together and make baby? You Jane, me Tarzan. He had four kids, no problem. His mother had seven kids, no problem. In fact, many of them were born in the kitchen in between bouts of scrubbing the floor. But the real clincher, the real confusion, began when we mentioned three simple letters—IVF.

We explained the entire in vitro fertilization process in the most layman terms possible not because Dad lacks intelligence but because he looked like a nervous wreck. "Dad, the sperm can't get to the egg so the doctors are going to remove these elements from our bodies and unite them in a petri dish. Then, if embryos develop, they'll put them back inside my uterus." He had that I-smell-bad-cheese look on his face as he forced a smile.

IVF—those innocent little letters were lingering in the air along with the smell of fresh garlic, pasta and parmesan (maybe it was bad cheese?). Like the garlic itself, we were afraid that these letters would repeat on him later that night when he had time to digest.

In the weeks to follow, he asked us how we were doing. Each time, he transformed "the IVF thing" into IBM, IGF, NBA, all kinds of incarnations. His acronyms were screwy but his message was always from the heart.

If he weren't so uncomfortable talking about the entire subject, a subject he felt completely unversed in, I imagine that he would reminisce with us, comparing today's world with the one he grew up and made babies in.

"I remember when a dirty water dog [hot dog] was five cents."

"In the old days you could stay out until all hours of the night without worrying about your safety."

"There was a time when couples made babies without even trying. IPX wasn't even a word back then."

In Dad's generation, which also happened to be my grandmother's generation, the "without even trying" babies were also called "oops" kids—a result of the drug store being fresh out of condoms. Today, an oops for a baby-making challenged couple means dropping a vial of medication all over the kitchen floor!

Still, no matter how impatient or angry you get when sharing your news with a person who gets a senior citizen discount, you mustn't lose faith. Don't lose your cool when they tell you that their mucus is hostile too. (Hey, they've been hacking up that same phlegm ball for 50 years, so to them, it is hostile!) Don't get agitated when they ask about your next urine sample. Don't blow your stack when they look at you like you're from another planet. They're doing everything they can to understand the weirdest phenomenon since television.

SECTION II: BABY STEPS

Initial Consultations and Testing

Ob-gyn and the "Delivery"

Obstetrician-gynecologists, or ob-gyns used to conjure up all kinds of yummy thoughts in my mind.

For years, women like us sought them out for the "gyn" part, taking care of general girlie maintenance. Breast examinations, Pap smears, infections, stuff like that. And the "ob" part always dangled before us, reminding us that one day these doctors would deliver our babies. Like bakers pulling fresh little loaves right out of the oven, obstetricians have been thought of as people who would eventually deliver fluffy, pleasant things into our lives.

But for many baby-making challenged couples, the ob-gyn is often the first person to deliver bad news.

So, maybe you've been trying to conceive for years and you decide it's time to start investigating the situation. Where do you begin? A trip to the ob-gyn, of course.

Where else would you begin? Not a full-fledged fertility specialist. No way. That would be too bold and too scary. Besides, going to the ob-gyn still feels normal. You haven't graduated to a deeper issue. No, not yet. And, that trip to the ob-gyn is still filled with hope. Maybe you'll conceive on the drive in.

The ob-gyn can help you to determine lots of things. Seems silly, but the first thing she might do is give you a pregnancy test. I'm convinced this is really to test how tough you are. I distinctly remember booking an appointment, telling the receptionist that I'm having trouble conceiving, and boom, the moment I arrived, they asked me to pee on a stick.

If your pregnancy test comes back negative, then, the doctor may run blood tests to check hormone levels—progesterone, estrogen, stuff like that. If there is nothing abnormal with these tests, the doctor may move onto her next victim: husband.

And what does he do? Basically, he gets to orgasm in a cup. A semen specimen is whisked off to a laboratory for analysis. If all looks good with the sperm, Dr. Ob-gyn is sure to return to the female anatomy, checking the inside mechanisms for blockages, scar tissue or any other obstruction that could be causing a problem. However, if like in our case, the semen analysis comes back flawed, hubby continues to receive his share of poking and prodding.

But do not despair if your ob-gyn delivers any unfavorable news. So, maybe she's lost her caché for the moment. Just think of this news as the first of deliveries she will make in your life. She's just working her way toward the mother of all deliveries—your baby.

Eye/Hand Coordination: The Semen Analysis

You men aren't very good at collecting your own semen.

Well, you used to be when you were twelve or thirteen years old. Back then, you did it so quietly and secretly in the bathroom that you never had time to think. Not that you collected it but you did one bang-up job of releasing it.

Just a few quick strokes, a mental picture of your homeroom teacher (boy, was she hot) and boom.

Or maybe you did it in your sleep. Not that you intended to. Waking up to wet sheets always put you in a sticky situation.

Then you grew older and found a couple of girls to do the dirty work for you. The high school tramp who helped everyone out. The college chick you said you loved who reciprocated with a gentle touch.

The girl you married.

Suddenly, she was in charge. The CEO (Chief Ejaculate Officer). Took care of all kinds of jobs. Took the job right out of your hands. For years, she ran the show and you loved it. No need for you to go back to old ways.

Until you were faced with the baby-making challenge.

Suddenly, the job is your job again. And your goal is more than feeling orgasmic. You're trying to produce the goods for a baby. The time has come—you have to take matters into your own hands again.

Say hello to the semen analysis. Of course, the people at the laboratory didn't mention that you could have had your significant other help you out at home. No. You assume your sample has to be fresh from the source, bottled right here at Laboratory Spring.

The nurse hands you a sterile cup and a sheet with 32 labels, each featuring your name, address, social security number and date of birth. Horror overcomes you: are they expecting 32 separate samples or are they willing to take your one contribution and divide it into 32 parts? You start doing the math in your head: one modest dollop divided into 32 parts equals a drop, a spritz, a mist, if you're lucky.

With the clean cup in one hand, a dirty magazine in the other and your pants around your ankles, you become thirteen again. If only they'd pipe in Mom's voice through the stereo speakers, it might speed things up.

Just as you're about to reach the top, you remember you need to bottle that happiness. You grab the sterile cup with one hand. Uh, no, the other hand. Good catch! Seal the jar shut, double-check all the names on the labels and pull your pants up.

For a brief moment you stare into the clear plastic container with its humbling measurement lines, thinking "That's it?" You've clammed bigger than that. Not to worry. Quality, not quantity, definitely counts in this scenario.

Walk with dignity to the front desk where you hand off your handiwork. Smile. Fix your eyes on the door behind you and walk straight out. You may be thinking the entire waiting room is talking about what you just did, but really, everyone is too wrapped up in what they're about to do to even notice you're in the room.

The Poop On the Goop

Let's start with the proper terms.

Semen is the fluid containing sperm and secretion from the testicles, prostate and seminal vesicles that is expelled during ejaculation.

Sperm is one part of the fluid and is known as the male gamete or reproductive cell.

The terms are so technical. And the seriousness of the tests and procedures makes men use formal expressions they'd never use under normal circumstances.

Guys, have you been talking like this? "Doctor, you need a semen specimen today? Well, we've abstained from relations for three days. And our prior relations were all completed with barriers. So, yes, I feel completely prepared to produce the specimen needed."

What men really want to say is cum.

After they've given semen for analysis they're really thinking they've shot their wad while whacking off or spanking the monkey.

While waiting the recommended two to three days to store up a healthy supply for the next episode of relations, men are really thinking how their balls are going to explode if they don't do the nasty already.

Formerly dick or man, they now refer to him as penis.

Joe Nuts, meet Señor Testicles.

Scrotes have been transformed into scrotum.

Rubbers are condoms and barriers.

Baby-making challenges, such as those issues involved with sperm (male factor is the term; not Max Factor, like the make-up), can quickly transform guttural male talk into technical, grown-up vocabulary.

The total sperm concentration (a.k.a. "swimmers"), which is the number of sperm in the ejaculate, can range anywhere from 20 to 200 million per ejaculate. Talk about ballparking it. While some men may have only a few million or even a few thousand, remember, ultimately all it may take to make a baby is one.

A semen analysis looks at more than just the count. It also looks at the volume, concentration, movement (motility) and size and shape of each sperm (morphology). Semen cultures may test for infections or other sperm busters that may be getting in your way.

Your doctor may be performing myriad semen analyses in order to get data on your ejaculate but, really, it's all about getting the poop on the goop that comes out of your pickle.

The Urologist and the Terrible Two's

For baby-making challenged couples, particularly the male counterpart, the terrible two's are a pair of testicles awaiting examination by a urologist.

I remember the look on my husband's face moments before meeting with this specialist of the male reproductive tract. He had read about this first examination—which would include feeling the scrotum for a varicocele (a varicose vein in the nut. Sorry, testicle)—and wondered what the doctor was going to do to his, you know, his boys.

I mean, if my husband couldn't see or feel any varicose veins in his testicles, if *I* couldn't see or feel them, then *how* the heck would the doctor get a fresh perspective?

My husband was white as the sheet wrapped around his waist. Scared as he was, he preferred that I leave the examination room. In his macho mind, his manhood was about to be tested and I was not invited to witness.

Since the day we had agreed we could be faced with a baby-making challenge, we had started all kinds of exploratory tests and procedures. My husband knew, for this particular one, the balls were in his court.

I listened by the door. Mumbles of small talk. Sudden silence. My husband's nervous cough. The doctor's voice. It was the longest ten minutes he ever endured. (My husband, that is.)

When he returned to the waiting room, looking sweaty and flushed, all he could say was "I feel violated."

What a baby. Women go through this kind of stuff all the time. Just a different angle.

Driving home, he could barely describe the squeezing, pulling and repositioning that went on in that tiny examination room.

Lisa Safran

A few day's later, the doctor's report concluded that there was a very small varicocele—too small to require surgery or to be causing our male factor (low count, low motility, abnormal morphology).

What's a couple to do?

A Cute, Little Bottom:
Boxers Versus Jockeys

In this corner, straight from your underwear drawer, weighing in at a light cotton blend, the one, the only, the favorite snug and sexy briefs . . . theeee jockey shorts. (Penis roars.)

And in this corner, the newcomer, a controversial contender against the reigning champion. He's light on his feet, he's airy, breezy . . . heeee's boxer shorts! (Testicles and millions of sperm cells cheer in delight.)

As long as I can remember, jockeys have been worn by young sexy guys with a six-pack of abs. Boxers were for out-of-shape Dads drinking a six-pack of beer.

But over the last few years boxers have become cool. And for those men whose sperm count is not up to par, boxers are even cooler because cool, loose environments tend to promote the production of healthier sperm.

Upon hearing about my husband's male factor, we packed up all of his skimpy jockey shorts and purchased loose, baggy boxers, three to a pack. Some were striped, some checked, most plain old white. Style and sex appeal took a back seat. Ventilation was key.

As per the urologist's recommendation (and all the stuff we'd been reading), we built our own cooling system for his steamy semen sacks by switching to boxers. Plenty of cross-ventilation from one wide leg to the other. CAC—central air for the crotch.

If his "boys" could talk to each other regarding this boxer shorts/jockeys issue, I'd imagine their conversation going like this: "Hey, chief, how do you like this new freedom the two of us got? No more sweating, slapping or chafing. I'm lovin' it."
"Yeah, dude. I used to hate that clammy feeling about midday. Glad it's over."

Upon hearing their conversation, the "main man" pokes his nose in. "Boxers give me a little too much freedom, if you know what I mean, fellas. And quite honestly, we're all interacting with one another more than I prefer!"

His man and his boys, conversing on the topic of undies. The jockey/boxer issue. Men and their genitalia have been talking about the controversy since the topic of fertility became chic but, still, many men and their underwear are torn.

If the controversy has got your shorts riding up, then why not liberate yourself with no undies at all?

Warm Bottles and Other Cool Ways to Empower Yourself

When it comes to a man's testicles and the production of sperm, heat is bad. It's not like a vegetable garden where the more sunshine the better the crop thrives. No, these bulbs seek shade and flourish in cool climates.

My husband was determined to try everything and anything to cool his coupling. The switch to boxer shorts was not enough for him. One night I saw him in front of the TV, pants completely off as a slow stream of cold air rose from his crotch. As I stood closer I could see a bag of frozen peas pressed up against his pee-pees. He was icing his nuts!

Actually, I thought this was a smart idea and an obvious sign of true dedication. Here it was, the middle of winter, and he was freezing his nuggets off in hopes of lowering the temperature of his testicles. (And he doesn't even like peas.) He knew that lower scrotal temperatures could help the quality of his semen. Seeing him in that vulnerable position gave the old drinking expression "on the rocks" an entirely new meaning . . . plus, it gave me a new appreciation for his commitment to our future baby.

It's important to keep the unit cold but the out*come* should remain warm. There were a few mornings when hubby produced the specimen at home and then braved the city traffic, hoping to get to the lab before the sample got too cool. To insulate it, he wrapped the specimen cup in tin foil and then placed it into a thick sweatsock, stuffing the entire package into his jacket pocket. It looked like a mini-science project. And once he arrived at the lab, he had to go through the embarrassment of the unveiling—yanking the package out of his pocket, peeling back the sock, unfolding the foil as if he were about to reveal a hot baked potato. It was a humbling experience.

In another attempt to "take the situation into our own hands," hubby began experimenting with Chinese herbs. The day he brought home tea leaves made from sparrow brain is when I decided to intervene. He got a tip from a non-English-speaking herbalist—tea, made from sparrow brain, could increase sperm count. How he got the tip without speaking the same language still baffles me.

I believe in natural, holistic remedies—ginseng, astragalus root, teas—but brain? Brain is not an herb, it's a body part. To me, brain was risky. And the fact that all the instructions on the box were written in Chinese (literally) was not a good sign. Besides, how intelligent is a puny little sparrow anyway and why would I want to brew a batch of tea from its gray matter?

Trying different creative remedies can be a wonderfully empowering method for taking control of your baby-making challenge, but be sure the instructions are written in your first language before diving in.

Mourning Sickness: Coming to Terms with Your Challenge

How can this be happening to us? Why us? This is not fair. Why can't we make a baby like a normal couple?

Sometimes, particularly when you're beginning to come to terms with your baby-making challenge, it's hard to get away from the "why" mentality. Your questions are good ones, and I too, often asked them of myself and my husband. But good questions don't always warrant good answers, or any answer at all.

That's just the way it is. Life is not always fair. And some people are chosen to face certain challenges because the person upstairs knows they *can*. (Geez, I sound like a mother already.)

Give yourself time to mourn. You both deserve it. Shed tears, get angry, bicker, eat gallons of ice cream, the works. But don't wallow in negativity for too long. Set a limit on your mourning period: no longer, let's say, than the amount of time it takes to get an appointment with a fertility specialist. Consider that period down time turned into productive down-in-the-dumps time.

It could be one month, two months, sometimes as much as three months. Anything more than that could be hazardous to your health and not even remotely funny.

Then, continue to take steps!

SECTION III: NEXT STEPS

Time To See the "Baby Doc"

Doing Your Homework

Welcome to the "next steps" stage. At this point, it is important to continue educating yourselves and taking control of your baby-making challenge. One of the most empowering things you can do, before going to see the "baby doc," is your homework.

Become a researcher, a librarian, a roving reporter. Collect all the information you possibly can and you'll feel less like a victim, more like an active participant in the treatment you're about to endure.

One of the best forms of research can be done on the Internet and for a few reasons. You can do it in the privacy of your own home, wearing pajamas, a bathrobe or nothing at all. You don't have to brush your hair or your teeth. You can sit back at the computer and let it all hang out.

Your significant other can lean over your shoulder or pull up a chair and you can perform your search together. You can talk as loudly as you want. You can become real emotional, if you feel the need. And you can shout out every four-letter word you know each time your computer crashes. No library will stand for these shenanigans.

Take it from me, someone who is a far cry from an Internet whiz, there are many ways to obtain pertinent information on the web.

If you perform a simple keyword search, try typing in the obvious: "fertility" and "infertility." (Those diabolical sister words return!) Up will pop a few billion options to peruse. Now, don't panic. If you look at a thousands listings each night you should be completed with your search in thirty years or so. Seriously, it's the art of perusing that you must master. Learn to skim information with one eye while the other eye carefully reads what pertains to your challenge. You might feel cross-eyed by the end of your search, but you'll be all the wiser.

Of course, you can log on to specific web sites for more specific information. The trick is knowing their names and who they are. To give you a jumpstart, I've provided you with a list of web sites worth visiting at the back of this book.

From those web sites, you will discover links. Not missing, sausage or chain but links that will bring you to other web sites that might be of interest to you. Perhaps this digging process will try your patience but you truly can learn a lot.

If you find yourself stuck in Internet overload, log off for awhile and continue doing your homework conventional ways. Spend a few hours in the local bookstore, reading and sipping coffee. Maximize the reference section of the library. (Just don't shout out any of those four-letter words you called your computer.) Even consult with the latest medical journals for breakthrough information on new techniques, procedures and studies. Ask your librarian for help getting started. Treat the process like the time when you wrote your high school paper on World War II. Collect all the information you can, take notes, set up specific folders and do not plagiarize.

Other ideas for obtaining info are talking to people who've "already been there." Chances are you already know someone who has been through, or is going through, a similar process. Muster up the courage to talk to them. Seek out advice, get tips. Feed your quest for knowledge as if you were in the process of buying a house, leasing a car or any other major event in your lives that requires an informed decision.

Try calling fertility centers around the country for different perspectives on similar processes. When you place these calls, tell each center that you're in the process of choosing a fertility group and that you'd like them to send you all the written information they can. If a country-wide search is too broad and overwhelming, just start with the groups in your vicinity. If a vicinity-wide search is still too broad at this stage of your process, just start with the center down the road.

Once you've made a good dent in your homework and you have the name of the fertility specialist you'd like to see, book your appointment.

Say "Hi" At Your Initial Consultation

If your first face-to-face with your fertility specialist feels like a job interview, don't be alarmed. It's perfectly normal.

Try to book your appointment before work, after, or on your lunch hour, so that you and your spouse are dressed presentably and professionally. First impressions are important. You want to look like grown-ups who are responsible enough to have kids. At a first interview, sweatpants and t-shirts don't cut it.

Upon meeting the doctor, give him a firm handshake, maintain eye contact, sit up straight in those stiff leather chairs and try to look relaxed. This is your first interview; you have a right to be nervous, but just try not to show it.

Small talk first. Where you're from. Former experience. Referrals. He'll be glancing at your paperwork in between questions. Answer his queries without making it obvious that you're searching for wall diplomas, personal family photos and other clues that might lead you to guess what type of bedside manner he has. While you scope out the office, try not to make it too obvious that you and your partner are kicking each other under the table.

Since this is your first interview together, it could last for a good 20-30 minutes, sometimes longer. You'll discuss your qualifications as a couple, the doctor's credentials and when next steps could begin. Chances are you won't report for duty that Monday but he'll at least want to give you a rough estimate of when new hires like you are starting.

Once the doctor sits back and slides his big chair a few inches away from the desk, consider yourself in. He is beginning to relax and so should you; the tough part of the interview is over.

Of course he'll ask you if you have questions and, like any good interviewee, you should answer "yes." Now's not the time to get shy. The two of you have been pondering and wondering for months now. In fact, you were just whispering your questions to each other in the waiting room. Speak up!

Once the interview is over, you will be given a "next step"— a date with his nurse, a meeting with the financial manager, a follow-up meeting with him. Congrats, you got the job!

Last I checked, the rules of etiquette said no follow-up thank you letter is necessary.   Just be prepared to get to work.

Go to Your Room (The Waiting Room, That Is)

Stepping into your fertility specialist's office for the first time is like a trip to the local Chinese take-out.

Like the photographs of edible dishes hanging on the walls at Hunan Whatever, you'll come face to face with dozens of treats your future doctor has whipped up.

Boys. Girls. Twins. Triplets. Babies in Santa hats. Babies in birthday suits. Babies in the arms of the doctor you're anxiously waiting to see. Don't they look yummy.

Ooo honey, check out that mouthwatering shot of Moo "Goo-Goo" Gai Pan. Or those twin lobster tails. They're probably a lot of work to crack but how satisfying those two must be. Hey, how about the Happy Family? Now there's a dish that sounds delish.

Together, you point and smile at the various delicacies, whispering little expletives until the receptionist finally calls your name.

"Ready to place your order?"

"Yes, please. We'd like the #4 special, you say, raising a finger toward an adorable cherub on the wall behind you. No MSG."

You hope the color photographs haven't given you a false picture of the chef's cooking abilities. Your stomach rumbles, your mind races and you pray that you or your spouse is in possession of the right cooking ingredients.

But once the novelty of staring at cute baby photos on the walls has worn off and you return to your doctor for subsequent visits, you'll start focusing on other things: the patients sitting around you.

While you wait for any given appointment—whether it be a quick blood draw, ultrasound, chat with the nurse or paperwork follow-up—you'll find yourself waiting and watching and checking one another out.

Some of us will smile at each other. You know, that show-no-teeth grin that you can barely muster so early in the morning. Others will stare straight into the television, avoiding eye contact at all costs. You could sit on that stone-faced woman's lap and she wouldn't even acknowledge you.

Of course, you'll see your share of couples. But most guys, if you look deep into their eyes, appear nervous and uncomfortable. Sure, the women appear that way, too, but the men have a different look of puzzlement. Like they inadvertently stepped into the ladies' room during intermission. Because the bottom line is: no matter where your baby-making challenge stems from—whether it be male factor or female factor—the ladies still get the brunt of the treatment! Girls, we know that and, boys, so do you! No wonder men have that funny look on their faces.

You also get those patients who bring their babies. Either they're suffering from secondary infertility (when everything went OK with the first baby but now, with the second, there's something wrong), or they're babysitting, or they just borrowed a friend's child in order to make everyone else feel miserable and jealous.

Everyone will respond to these miniature people differently. I, for one, usually grow that dopey "I'm looking at a kid and I want one, too" grin. Like Miss America, I could hold that silly smile for hours if the baby stuck around. But others will sneer at the Mom for bringing in her bundle of joy. "How dare you flaunt that little thing around here when all of us are suffering. Can't you see we're suffering!" (OK, we're suffering.)

Once you've had enough of people-watching, you can focus your attention on the stack of magazines you've read from cover to cover at least three times. Actually, you never really did read them. You just pretended to read them while you were checking everyone out.

And while we're on the subject of waiting rooms, they can be viewed as a reflection of the treatment you're about to get at your fertility center of choice.

I remember my first affiliation with a reproductive center. The waiting room was outside of the office, in front of the elevator. Basically, it was the hallway. I guess that negates the entire concept of "room." If there is just a row of chairs lined up against the wall in front of the elevator, the waiting room is nothing more than a waiting area. Room versus area—it's a world of difference.

Because if you're asked to sit in a waiting area, you're stripped of all pride and dignity. In my waiting area experience, I sat in an old, beat-up chair (on days I was lucky enough to get a seat) watching the up/down elevator button light for an endless 25 minutes. I desperately avoided looking at the people who came off the elevator as they walked away from the massive sign that said "Reproductive Center." Why not place three scarlet letters—"IVF"—on my sweater and we'll call it a day?

The waiting area was void of magazines, coffee tables (actually, if you don't have magazines, who needs tables?) and a discreet bathroom. The john was smack in the middle of the waiting area so whatever you did in there everyone else heard about.

However, I didn't remain at this waiting-roomless reproductive center for very long. For the few months I was affiliated with that group, I did receive decent care, but not until I stepped into a waiting *room,* a virtual palace, did I realize how much better things could be.

There it was, a place of beauty. Rows and rows of matching chairs, walnut tables glistening with a lemon-fresh Pledge shine, complimentary coffee and more than one bathroom situated in a quiet little corner. Now that's what I call a waiting room!

I was more than happy to spend 25 minutes in waiting rooms like this. Heck, leave me there all morning if you like. With coffee, reading materials and a comfy chair, I'm set.

In fact, I found myself drawn to the same chair over and over again as if I was sitting in my own living room. It didn't matter that all the chairs were the same. I had chosen my favorite one and I sat there any chance I got. Even if another woman was in my chair when I first arrived, I found myself waiting for her to head over to the bathroom so that I could hop into my comfort zone.

Of course, waiting rooms do not necessarily reflect the level of treatment of expertise you will receive from a particular group. All the waiting room can do for you is make waiting for those experts a little more pleasant. Therefore, take notice of how the chairs are situated. Look for a semi-circle grouping and stay clear of waiting areas with rows and rows facing the same direction (unless you're going for treatment at the movie theater or Department of Motor Vehicles).

Some waiting rooms of beauty will hang artsy pictures and sport a couple of TVs giving you staring options. And then there's the tropical fish tank bubbling happy, soothing thoughts into your psyche. Bloop, bloop, everyone here is calm and content. Blood, bloop, the doctor was called away to an emergency and won't return for hours. How delightful.

Your waiting room should be comfortable and pleasant because you may frequent it a few times each week, especially when your treatment kicks into full gear. You'll want it to feel like your second home, not like you want to run away from this home.

Carefully eye the layout. Take notice of the month (and year) of the latest *People* magazine. See if there is a TV or music or fish tank to help pass the time and fill the empty, quiet air. And most importantly, be sure that the waiting room has four walls and that you can't hear the toilet flushing from what will quickly become your favorite chair.

Grab a Crayon
and Sign Here

In our world—and I'm not talking about just the baby-making world, I'm talking the entire world—when you're dealing with something important you're usually faced with a sea of paperwork.

If you thought it was an important moment in your lives but there's no paperwork involved, think again. You could be falling into a faux-important situation.

Since the two of you have been one, you've experienced a flood of tests, licenses, policies, leases, contracts, closings, statements, wills, won'ts. I'm getting a cramp just thinking about it.

And now, as you embark on your baby-making challenge, you will once again be faced with a wave of waivers, a dose of documents and a ream of releases. It may seem alarming but it's all part of an "important situation" routine. So don't be discouraged by the piles of paperwork and the discussion of morbid issues. Think of these things as proof of how meaningful your challenge really is.

Cleaning Your Plate

As your heads get wrapped around doctor's appointments and confusing choices, don't forget to channel your energy into a baby-making challenged couple's most critical issue: taking care of each other.

In the old days (OK, that might be a long, long time ago, so think hard), before you even began talking about babies, perhaps even marriage, you both had fun together. As a new couple, there were fewer heavy-duty issues consuming your brains. You spent lots of time together. You listened to each other. You cared about each other. And you laughed. These are the things that made your relationship as strong as it is today.

Now, with a baby-making challenge in front of you, there are greater reasons to make time for one another. It's time you cleaned your plates.

Stop working 80-hour weeks. You need your rest. Don't worry, the work will still be there, piled high, once you've conquered your baby-making challenge.

Don't take on major tasks. Forget about building the second floor on your house, hold off on digging the hole for the swimming pool, put off training for the triathlon. You can achieve these ambitious goals some other time.

Spend less time with people you merely tolerate. We're all guilty of those dinners with "friends" we could do without, or family outings that leave you wishing you owned a gun. The point is to *spend* your time with others, not waste it. Be selective and don't worry about what they'll think of you. You and your spouse are beginning a very important chapter in your lives. If, under your breath, you're mumbling "what a dope this guy is," then perhaps he's one person to avoid. Instead, hang out with people who make you feel good, and of course, who make you laugh.

Spend more time with each other. You may not be able to get away to the Caribbean but at least you can carve out time, just for the two of you. Tell friends you're going somewhere far away for the weekend, and even if you can't get away, lock yourselves in the house for two days. Go for walks together and be sure to hold hands. Play board games, rent movies, have thumb wrestles, anything that will give you an excuse to strengthen the powerful bond that's already there but may have been weakened by your baby-making challenge.

Screen your phone messages. Those people whom you merely tolerate could be calling. And don't forget to jam the doorbell. Those intolerable folk could be standing on your doormat right now.

Clean your plate of all extraneous stuff and you will find yourself feeling stronger, more rested and more prepared for the challenges ahead.

SECTION IV: BIG STEPS

Further Testing, Examining, Poking and Probing

But First, a Tribute to Future Mommies

You're either on your way to figuring out what's causing your baby-making challenge or you've already nailed it. Now, before we get too deep into the different experiences you could be enduring, let's take a moment to pay tribute to the future mommies of the world. (What are looking behind you for? I'm talking about you!)

The reason we need to pay tribute to you is because no matter what your baby-making challenge is, you are going to get the physical brunt of it all. We women are here to bear pain. Probably because we can, which is why you will be giving birth to your future baby, not hubby.

As you know by now, in my case, male factor was our problem but the most *physical* discomfort hubby had to go through was aiming his ejaculation into a cup and not all over the bed. Whether you, too, are experiencing male factor, or female factor (which could be anything from endometriosis to polycystic ovaries), you, the ladies, are going to deal with the physical discomfort and pain.

You will be poked and prodded, scanned and monitored. You will take hormone shots. You will get naked many mornings right after you've just gotten dressed at home. You will feel like a human pincushion. But you have the potential to give birth.

Since hubby will be feeling so bad watching you endure, he's sure to cater to your every whim. Get plenty of back massages, foot rubs, let him cook dinner as much as possible, leave the toilet scrubbing to his discretion. Milk it.

The Probing Pacifier

Sonogram or ultrasound—what's the difference?

Both refer to a diagnostic technique that uses sound waves, rather than X-rays, to visualize internal body structures. You could use either word and be correct—it's a matter of which one you choose. Seems to me, though, in our situation we shouldn't be given a choice. The medical profession is the expert here. We rely on them to tell us what is and what isn't. By having two words for the same procedure, we find ourselves caught in a mental struggle of which one to go with in a simple sentence.

Sonograms and ultrasounds can work two different ways. In the first, the doctor checks you internally with a probe. (And that's exactly what he's doing—probing.) The second method, and you've seen this on TV, is when the doctor rubs a transducer (good Trivial Pursuit word) across your stomach after squeezing a blob of gooey gel (not good Trivial Pursuit words) there. It's as if your stomach is a giant mouse pad and the doctor is moving the mouse around while watching the screen for the proper activity. This form of ultrasound is what many of us associate with pregnant woman so, girls, until we too are pregnant, be patient with the vaginal version. The vaginal sonogram can usually provide greater detail, so hang in there.

Back to the original question here—sonograms or ultra-sounds? I like the word sonogram because you can abbreviate it down to sono and sound medically cool. But the choice is totally up to you.

And speaking of sonos, don't you just love the condom that hangs off the probe as you sit there waiting for the doctor? There it is, just staring you in the face. Sticking straight up with an extra-strength

75

Trojan rolled halfway down. The probe is a magic wand and your doctor is the magician. It's the conductor's baton. The teacher's pointer. Moses' staff. Your pacifier.

Pacifier because you will find yourself relying on this instrument to tell you how you're responding to the treatments.

As you watch the screen, you can see your insides in black and white. (Hey, didn't anyone ever consider Technicolor? It's the 21st century, you know.) I remember seeing my ovaries right after hormone suppression. Black sleepy irregular blobs. They looked like little pussycats all curled up for a nap.

Just days later, after stimulation began, my ovaries were full and awake. Perky little buggers. A good nap does wonders.

Sonos will become one of your most common procedures. In fact, you'll find yourself looking forward to them as they provide a sense of security as well as a window to your reproductive system . . . and, if you're real deep, your soul.

Blood Exam Boo-Boos

When it comes to their children, parents talk about how they give blood every day. Well, when you're baby-making challenged, you get plenty of practice.

Your medical team will be monitoring your blood levels for a myriad of items: estradiol (estrogen), progesterone, hCG (a.k.a. the pregnancy hormone), you name it. Phlebotomists are a bunch of pleasant vampires in white coats.

And some of them know how to suck your blood better than others. There's the phlebotomist who can do it so painlessly you barely feel the needle hanging out of your arm. Conversely, there's the one who will slap your arm silly in search of a vein. Doesn't she realize the vein is hiding from her!

Some will strap the rubber strap around your arm so tightly you'll feel the circulation cutting off in your feet. Others will barely tie it and still are successful.

Some will have you remove your sweater and suit jacket. Others will practically do it right through your sleeve. Some will give you a band-aid. (Don't leave it on all day or your skin will get irritated.) Others will ask you to hold a blob of cotton there until lunchtime. Some will bruise you terribly, others will leave the tiniest boo-boo.

Some will talk to you about the weather, others will talk to you about the number of tubes they're filling up.

If you're squeamish (like me), take my advice and DO NOT WATCH! Turn your head the other way, close your eyes, make small talk or picture a beautiful tropical island where blood tests are banned by the government. And don't forget to breathe deeply.

Breathing is very important and many of us forget how to do it. Remember to breathe from your stomach (actually, your diaphragm, which is not to be confused with the one you used to wear for contraception) and not from your shoulders. Watch your belly rise as you breathe through your nose. These deep inhales/exhales will help calm you down, keep oxygen flowing and lower your blood pressure.

But deep breathing usually causes lots of wind in the face of the person drawing your blood. Be sure to brush your teeth before you leave the house for there's nothing worse than morning breath gusting in the face of an innocent bystander. If you had a cup of coffee on the drive in, then pop a mint or stick of gum. Remember, you don't want to offend or distract the person sucking tubes of blood out of your arm with noxious odors.

If you happen to be one of those people who are not blood-test phobic, then I've heard the best way to deal with frequent draws is to watch. Non-phobic people claim that watching can help them to feel more empowered and less like a victim, a submissive patient. (My, how I admire you folk. Watching would be the end of me, for sure!)

After your blood test is sent off to the lab for results, you should get a phone call (or you will be instructed to call the doctor's office) later that day. The findings will usually set the tone for the next 24 to 48 hours. Take more medications, cut back on medications, come in again tomorrow.

With all the blood you're losing, do you need to replenish with a thick juicy steak? Sure, why not. Go for a delicious filet mignon every once in a while. Frequent blood tests are a good excuse to dine out.

Another good thing about frequent blood tests, especially if you have always had a phobia (like some people I know), is that you get plenty of practice. The more blood I gave, the more confident I grew. OK, so maybe I still don't have the courage to watch but at least I no longer have to lie down afterwards, drink a quart of orange juice or be scraped off the floor by a team of nurses.

Cover Up Your Footsies

If you are going through the trials and tribulations of the baby-making challenge, you must invest in a critical piece of wardrobe: socks.

Socks will be worn everywhere and, quite often, worn completely and totally alone.

Therefore, they must always be clean. Never, ever have a hole. And match.

Stay clear of knee-highs (they look really dumb with those threadbare cotton robes). Forget about trouser-length socks (without the trousers, what's the point?). And please, please, never wear full-length pantyhose. (You'll eventually wind up in your bare feet. Bare feet and cold stirrups make for a wicked combination unless it's the middle of August.)

When choosing your sock wardrobe, may I suggest the following:

The Basic Black Sock: perfect for your first consultation, this shows you have class, elegance, a sense of style. Goes well with any examining room decor—contemporary, medical or that classic, cold metallic look.

School-Girl Anklets: basic and clean, these work well during any procedure. Whites and creams are preferable.

Knee Socks: these are particularly good in the winter, providing extra warmth to more of your leg. If worn with a plaid lap cloth, they give you that chic parochial-school or classic Scotsman look.

Scrunchies or Slouchies: for a more athletic look, go with these bulky sweatsocks pushed down low over the ankles. Perfect for laboratory procedures like biopsies when you want to shout out: "I'm not afraid. Give me your best procedure. And do it now!"

Designer Anklets: these may cost a little more but they work really well during a procedure in which you are knocked out cold. Take egg retrievals, for example. A designer anklet is a great way to make a statement when the last thing you remember doing was making a fist.

Theme Socks: if you're going to see your doctor on Halloween, wear black and orange jack-o-lanterns; red hearts are a real conversation piece on Valentine's Day. Try wearing one pink and one blue sock on the day you get your pregnancy test! A little imagination will provide comic relief for you and your medical team.

Go ahead—sock it to them!

Clap Hands and Keep Your Feet In the Stirrups

Having a pelvic exam is a lot like going on a first date.

The morning of the big day, I find myself an extra 15 minutes in the shower. Lathering up, shaving down, scrubbing every nook and cranny. Taking special care.

I choose my best white underwear. Nothing too sexy. (I don't want to give the wrong impression.) And I make sure the socks are clean, unholy and, of course, a matched pair. A scented panty liner ensures a trace of freshness when faced with summer heat, morning traffic and the dreaded case of nervous gas.

I'm told to slip into something way too comfortable for a humble girl like me. As the thin sheet drapes my squeaky-clean bod, I wait. Wait for my date. In the meantime, I keep checking and poking and peeking. (God forbid he should come in while I'm doing this.)

And then he walks in. Smiles and goes right for my chest to listen to my heartbeat. But when I hear that low stool wheeling my way, I know it's time. "Slide down," he says. Like I haven't heard that line before. I try to make small talk as his face disappears behind my cloaked legs. Could there be a piece of Charmin stuck there like a spinach blob between two teeth? What about the old fish market jokes? Maybe there's one going through his mind as he smears, pokes and probes.

He senses my discomfort. "Relax, I'm not going to hurt you." Pain is not the issue here. Some girls just never relax during one of these visits. It's like the awkward first time. Over and over again.

"OK, you can sit up." Such beautiful words. And I'm free to see his face again. Fortunately the look of disgust is not there. He discusses the details of the exam in a professional way while I'm thinking if all his patients are as neurotic as I am. Such a neurosis,

81

you'd think I'm a mess down there. Really, it's fine. Ask my husband. But maybe it's like when you think your house is in order until a friend comes over and is shocked by the chaos.

"Get dressed," he says. Sure, doc. The visit wasn't bad at all. I should be much more relaxed on our next date.

If only . . .

Gather 'Round—It's Time for Show and Tell

You'd be surprised by the amount of interesting conversation that occurs when people are huddled around your crotch.

Legs high, feet apart, vision impaired, all you really can rely upon is your auditory sense. It becomes so sharp, you could hear a sperm cell drop.

The doctor is talking to the nurse. The nurse is talking to another nurse. Your husband is talking to the doctor. And since you haven't had breakfast yet, your stomach is talking to whoever will listen. Occasionally, someone will talk to you. At least you think it's you. Then again, maybe it's her. Your crotch.

"I'm going to do a sonogram now. Relax your knees." The lights dim low and all I see is the condom-covered fluorescent green probe he's about to stick up my you-know-what. I feel like easy prey at an '80s discotheque.

The lights return.

"We're almost done. I just need to get enough tissue for the biopsy."

An endometrial biopsy is just one of the many procedures you may participate in. In my case, the doctor performed it to ensure the lining in my uterus was in tip-top shape. Quite honestly, I remember it as one of the more painful procedures but fortunately I was distracted by the conversation around me.

"Doctor, do you want me to prepare a Pap smear while you're there?"

Uncomfortable silence. Did that mean "yes" he wanted a Pap smear? Or was the lack of words his way of saying "no, thanks?" Maybe he gave her a nonverbal thumbs up or a high-five to clear the procedure.

"You know, Ms. Safran, you just reminded me of something I haven't thought of in 40 years." The doctor spoke. But oh, God, I thought. What could I be reminding him of? Something he hadn't heard of in four decades? Bearded women, the fish market he grew up near, what? He spoke again. "You just reminded me that I used to call my brother Sniffy."

Now I was panicking.

"Hearing you sniffle like that, I remembered my brother had allergies too and always sniffled. Sniffy, I called him."

Never mind about my hay fever. I was beginning to sweat.

"Hold still while I insert a thin tube. I need to understand the path to your uterus."

The path? I didn't know I had one. Is it like a hiking trail, marked with little color posts, or unmarked, a virtual jungle in there? All I knew was that this scoping procedure was called trial of transfer. Sounds like a test run for going from one bus to another. Should I ask any questions? I wasn't sure who he was talking to. Me, the nurse—or "her."

But once you do decide to speak up, you'll find you're saying the strangest things.

"You know, doctor," I said, "that part of a woman's body is supposed to be so sexy but, with all this traffic down there lately, it feels like Grand Central Station."

Then I segued to a bumbling "I never get used to these things, these examinations."

And for my final closing, "Did you hear the joke about the sperm cell, the follicle and the chicken?"

Take my advice, when the coffee crotch meets, whether it be daily, weekly or monthly, keep your legs open and your mouth closed. Something embarrassing is less likely to come out.

Silly Words Like
Ping Thing

Here's a procedure that's harder to say than it is to get: hysterosalpingogram.

Go ahead, try to say it. Not in choppy little syllables. Say it as one fluid word. I know, it's impossible.

Whenever my doctor talked about this procedure, I played the word association game in my head.

Ping pong.

Bingo!

Sal Pingram. (I went to college with him.)

Until I learned a trick. The folks at the radiology center called it an HSG. Aha, an acronym! That I could deal with!

Basically, an HSG is a dye test used to determine if a woman's uterus and fallopian tubes are normal and clear or if there are any blockages. It's one of many "ruling out" processes necessary for certain situations.

The way it works is simple. You get naked from the waist down (no biggie since you're used to that by now) and cloak yourself with a dignified sheet about the size of a large dinner napkin.

Lie down on a table while the doctor or technician combines small talk with technical info you legally need to know.

Then, pretend you're at a carnival playing that water squirt game. You know, the one when you shoot the water gun into the clown's mouth until the balloon fills up. A winner!

Only in this situation, the doctor has the gun, the balloons are your fallopian tubes and your private part is the clown. (Nice hair, Bozo).

Radiopaque dye, which is dye that the x-ray machine can pick up, is inserted through the cervix and uterus to see whether or not it spills out of the fallopian tubes into the pelvic cavity. Pretty much right after the dye is inserted, you may start to feel crampy and bloated. The x-rays are snapped as you shift from side to side while still lying flat on your back. The test usually lasts a few minutes. Before the test, your doctor may suggest that you take some mild pain killers in order to nip any pain in the bud. After the procedure, there's usually a bit of bleeding or spotting. And the crampiness may continue for a short while.

Sure, an HSG may be an uncomfortable procedure but just think of all the fun you can have making up silly little phrases that rhyme with ping thing.

SECTION V: JUMBO STEPS

Determining Your Plan
of Action and Plunging In

Sign Up for Day Care

By now, after your first few visits with the doctor, basic blood work, preliminary procedures and other fluid analysis, you may be lucky enough to know what's causing your baby-making challenge.

If so, you're ready to start day care.

Day care for baby-making challenged couples includes constant monitoring, nonstop interaction with the doctors and nurses, plus juice and cookies and an occasional nap. That's what happens when you participate in any technologically induced baby-making method.

In our case, we signed up at the IVF day care center.

We knew we had the goods to make a baby—it was just that the goods couldn't get close enough to each other for magic to happen.

My eggs were dropping each month, my tubes were crystal clear and his sperm were desperately trying to swim their way over, but they never made the full lap. Each month, the race began. His Johnny Weissmullers jumped off the diving board only to turn into little dog paddlers once they hit the waves. I'm sure they saw their destination on the horizon—ovary island—but the poor guys never made it. Millions of them, lost at sea.

Funny, my husband never learned to swim either.

For couples like us with male factor, there is a fabulous medical breakthrough that can jet ski the sperm right over to their destination—ICSI.

ICSI and Other
Labor Pains

ICSI (intracytoplasmic sperm injection), a specific treatment which can be used in IVF (in vitro fertilization), is a great option for BMCCWMF (baby-making challenged couples with male factor).

After the doctor explained the procedure, we were in awe. In the simplest explanation, a single sperm is injected right into an egg, the egg is fertilized, the embryo is placed into the uterine cavity and we pray for baby to form. Cool. Sign us up.

ICSI gave us hope and when you're baby-making challenged you need that. It completely worked around the problem that was causing our baby-making glitch. Hubby had enough healthy sperm but none of them could swim fast enough or long enough to make the long trek to the egg, naturally.

This breakthrough in technology is a clear case of someone brilliant out there identifying a problem and coming up with a solution. (Thank you, dear brilliant person!) In fact, it truly is breakthrough—breaking through the egg with an instrument in order to get the sperm where it should be. Micromanipulation, they call it. This was one time neither of us minded being manipulated.

ICSI and IVF fall under the umbrella of ART (assisted reproductive technology), and there are many other techniques you can participate in depending upon your unique situation, history, age and so on.

IUI (intrauterine insemination), when prepared sperm is inserted into the uterine cavity at the time of ovulation, is something we tried twice without success. Our doctor had told us there was about a ten percent chance of a pregnancy. Every baby-making challenged couple I've spoken to has tried this procedure and most without success. But I guess there's someone out there—a good ten percent—whom it will work for. I hope it's you!

IUI seems to be a "get your feet wet" procedure—a way of getting used to artificial means before diving full force into more aggressive treatment like IVF. Kind of like foreplay. A way of getting primed, pumped and completely in the mood for more intense stuff.

In fact, stay with me here as I further explore the sex analogy.

IVF, which is fertilization outside of the body, can be viewed as sex in the broadest term. The orgasm. Then, within the world of sex, we have the following techniques. GIFT (gamete intrafallopian transfer) combines the egg with the sperm and then places the egg/sperm combination directly into the fallopian tube where, hopefully, natural conception will occur. GIFT is like stimulating your private parts before the actual act so that natural intercoital orgasm can take place.

Then there's ZIFT (zygote intrafallopian transfer), where the egg and the sperm are united and, once the egg fertilizes (known as a zygote), it is transferred into the fallopian tube. ZIFT takes the GIFT stimulation one step further by achieving "climax" with artificial means (use your imagination, please), skipping actual sex altogether and then lying in each other's arms.

You may consider Blast, which is when embryos are placed back into the uterus at five days, the blastocyte stage, instead of the typical three days. Imagine this as oral sex for women—it takes longer for results to happen.

Some of these techniques can be used together, depending upon how kinky you two are. Consult your physician.

The Curriculum: A Quick Overview of an IVF Cycle

From now until the end of the book I will share with you the many different aspects involved in an in vitro fertilization cycle. Although there is a certain universal message here about IVF and ART procedures in general, remember that these stories are based on my own experiences.

Before getting into each specific area of my cycle, here's a quick run-down of the events that occurred; events that could happen to you, too.

Pre-cycle day 1: Get period. Chances are, you will be instructed to call the doctor's office to report the onset of menses. Your schedule can now be finalized. In a few days, you should begin your hormone suppressing shots. These shots may continue every day until your next period . . . and perhaps, beyond.

Cycle day 1: Get next period—hopefully, your last one for a very long time! Call the doctor's office to report the onset of menses. Your schedule can now be finalized.

Cycle day 3: Blood work and sonogram to confirm the quieting of your ovaries, the shedding of endometrium (lining of the uterus) and the readiness of a new cycle. Begin hormone stimulation shots. Continue shots until otherwise advised by your medical team. You will be called back to the doctor's office for frequent blood work and sonograms.

Cycle day 12: hCG shot (this day varies depending on each individual's response to medications). Once your follicles (there could be a broad range of numbers growing—single digit to a few dozen!) have reached optimal maturity, your medical team will tell you precisely what time to give yourself the hCG shot. All hormone suppressing and stimulating shots are usually stopped at this time.

(The following cycle days are based on a day 12 hCG shot)

Cycle day 13: more blood work, perhaps a sonogram. Your only shot free day in a long time! Enjoy it!

Cycle day 14: egg retrieval. This is when you undergo aspiration of your follicles to obtain your eggs. Usually, you are out cold for this out-patient surgery. Afterwards, you may start progesterone shots, continuing them until otherwise advised by your medical team.

Cycle day 17 (or 19, depending upon protocol): egg transfer. Your babies are placed inside your endometrial cavity and you are usually awake for this spectacular out-patient procedure.

Cycle day 21 (or about): blood work.

Cycle day 5,000,000 (well, that's how long it feels): blood work—this is your pregnancy test!

Now that you have a general idea of the timeframe of one person's experience with an IVF cycle, let's get into some specific observations worthy of a smile.

A Bundle of Meds

Preparing a woman's body for an IVF cycle is like turning her into a human hormone warehouse.

You know, those places were everything comes in bulk. And everything is bigger than normal size. Mega is the motto.

The doctor helps you to chart when to begin planning the store. First, clear the shelves of any old, expired or defective merchandise. Daily shots of a hormone suppressants will empty the shelves known as ovaries.

Then, once the shelves are stripped as clean as they can get, you'll start stocking up. Hormone stimulants will help you pack the shelves with more eggs than your ovaries will feel they can hold. Every few days, your doctor will take inventory, making sure that your goods are sufficient.

At one point, the eggs will be yanked from the shelves, fertilized and then placed back on a different shelf down aisle uterus. In retail, they call this repackaging. Whichever eggs (well, really embryos) you don't use at that time may be stored away in the frozen section.

Being a human warehouse has its pluses and minuses. The stocking-up process is wonderful and it gives you a sense of security that you're not going to run out of these "staples" any time soon. If you should lose a couple of eggs in the process, it's nice to know you have a healthy supply to fall back on.

But being a human warehouse also comes with side effects. You know how cranky you get wandering through those crowded stores? Up and down the aisles, not sure if you'll ever find what you came in there for? Well, hormone suppression and stimulation can cause the same irritable feeling. And the prices—quantity does not come cheap! Plus, you could be purchasing all these goods in bulk without really knowing about the quality until much later at the retrieval stage.

When it's your turn to become a human hormone warehouse, view your experience as a clearance sale. It doesn't happen too often, it won't last for very long and all sales are final.

Shotty Training:
Learning How to Give
Yourself Shots

My theory is that people who never went to medical school purposely avoided becoming a doctor because they couldn't stand the sight of blood, needles or dissecting a cat. Few of us could face the junior high school frog. So we turned to other careers where it wasn't mandatory to hold a surgical instrument steady in our hands.

And now here we are with a syringe in those same shaky hands, getting ready to perform weeks, perhaps months, of shots, not on poor little lab animals—but on ourselves.

My particular reproductive center required that all IVF participants take an injection therapy class. And it's a good thing because, quite honestly, we were clueless.

I was expecting an evening of "how-to" tips but, by the end of the three-hour crash course I felt as if I was going to perform open-heart surgery—when just last week I had trouble removing a splinter.

Six innocent couples sat around a large conference table as the head nurse led us into shot-dom. We started with a brief overview of the next few weeks we were about to endure and then dove into the nitty-gritty of needles.

First, the nurse passed out a care package to each couple. In it, we found a semi-long needle, a really long needle, a freakin' huge needle, alcohol swabs, a vial of saline solution, a chuck (the nickname for Charles, or an absorbent pad) and an orange. What, no candy? It was a Halloween goodie bag minus the goodies.

We spread the chuck out first, lined up all of our tools on top and placed the citrus fruit dead center. Then the nurse took us through each step.

Crack open the glass vial of saline but be sure to press away from the blue indicator dot. (Otherwise you could cut your finger, get glass in the solution or both.)

Pull the syringe back to 1 cc (that's the black line next to the number 1 and, no, it doesn't stand for "carbon copy"). Clean the vial top with an alcohol swab. Plunge needle into rubber vial top. Push air out of syringe. Hold vial upside down (but not totally upside down, more like on an angle).

Draw syringe back to 1 cc again. Pull needle out of vial. Flick out air bubbles (because you don't want to inject air into your body). Grab orange. Dart needle into the fruit (which is representative of your butt). With one hand, hang onto the needle while the other hand pulls back on the syringe checking for blood. If no blood (or orange juice, in this case), depress syringe top with your thumb until all fluid is expelled into the orange. Pull needle out quickly. Use an alcohol swab to apply pressure to the orange. A snap!

As we concentrated on performing each step with precision, I eavesdropped on the other couples.

"Shoot! I cut myself!"

"Goddamn needle. I just poked my thumb."

"How the f—k am I supposed to know what I'm doing?"

"I can't do this. Let's get a puppy."

Everyone was moaning and one couple grabbed their coats and walked out.

The nurse continued to share her years of wisdom while reminding us that this particular practice run was a simulation of intramuscular progesterone shots (shots in the bootie). We would still need to master other techniques for subcutaneous shots (tummy or thigh shots), those that would require mixing powder and saline together. The latter was a much more complicated process. And when were we going to cover these steps, I thought. In the graduate course?

Next, we were handed a pamphlet of medication descriptions along with side effects to watch for. The class grew quiet, feeling overwhelmed, helpless, basically like a group of adult fools. It was time for a coffee break. We drank our refreshments, stared at one another and pretty much all agreed that we were screwed.

For the last hour of class, the nurse went over more paper-work—from telephone lists and who to call with which questions to each individual couple's start date. Start dates were based on the first day of each woman's next menstrual cycle. Whatever date that was represented the moment each couple would begin. Sure, put the pressure on us girls.

My start date was July 18, 1998, a few weeks from the day of this injection therapy class. Eons away. In those weeks our mem-ories could dull considerably. We could totally forget how to check the needle for blood. Or completely block out how to break open the vials. We were brain-dead that very night—imagine what six weeks of nerves was going to do for us.

The 9:00 p.m. bell rang and class was dismissed, set free into a world of shot experimentation where we'd all be doing the same thing to our bodies as we just did to that poor orange. We had grad-uated, but with what kind of schlock diploma?

In just a few short weeks, this average group of stressed-out folk would pretend to be as skilled as a group of qualified nurses.

But we were really shaking in our booties.

Cuddle In a Cozy Spot
and Give a Shot

We are creatures of habit and when we don't know what we're doing—like giving ourselves shots—habit can be even more comforting.

Take location, for example. Choosing the same physical place to administer all of your shots can be quite soothing. But think twice before making this decision. Here are some thoughts to keep in mind.

Avoid large, blind-less windows. At some point your bare behind will be in your partner's face. Do you really want the neighbors to see this?

Look for ample counter space. A dining room table, a kitchen counter, your desk—any place that provides a vast amount of space without excess clutter. There's nothing worse than accidentally wiping your rear end with a wad of scrap paper instead a swab of alcohol.

Position yourself near a firm chair. You'll probably be getting a good number of shots in your leg or stomach and it's easier to give them if you're sitting down. A big, cushy chair tends to cause sinkage and if you're too deep into the cushions you're going to have trouble sticking it to yourself. Beanbag chairs, beach chairs and director's chairs, although all highly stylish, are not recommended. Another firm seat you may find comfy is the toilet. (Seat down, please.)

Stay clear of mirrors. Don't stand in front of the vanity unless you're one of those sick, kinky people who get off watching self-afflicting acts.

Seek out proper lighting. Candlelit rooms are delightful if you're setting a calm and seductive mood. But without the proper lighting the shots may wind up in your partner's butt instead of your own.

Be near the phone. After your first shot, you'll probably want to call someone just to let the world know you did it. The night of your follicle-releasing hCG shot, you may get panicky and will want to page your doctor. Or you may just get hungry and decide to call in a pizza. Cordless phones provide a good option. Take them along before sticking it to you.

Set up a needle drop. If you can find yourself a sterile syringe container, then position it in a discreet corner near your shot spot. Otherwise, make use of large freezer bags, old Easter baskets and last season's purse. (Just don't forget where you're putting them!)

Choose your shot spot wisely and you will find comfort in knowing there is a safe and familiar place to go to do your daily thing . . . a place the neighbors can't see from their bedroom window.

Break Open
the Piggy Bank

We all know that raising a child is expensive—formula, clothes, toys, diapers, bicycles, cars, college tuition. In our situation, having a child, just producing that little bundle of joy, can cost a small fortune, too.

If you have good medical coverage, you're probably set, at least for 80% of the entire undertaking. However, if you don't have proper coverage or if your insurance carrier is rather slippery about what they do and do not cover, then crack open the piggy bank.

Start checking under the sofa cushions. Pick up those pennies abandoned on the sidewalk. Grab a shiny metal cup and start begging because the costs are astronomical.

I'm not complaining and neither are you—I'm just stating the facts. And the facts can be staggering: doctor visits, blood work, hormones, syringes, needles, prenatal vitamins, antibiotics, alcohol swabs, plus don't forget all those meals at the local diner or Chinese take-out. Many couples who are baby-making challenged rarely like to cook at home. A good number of us are too tired to shop for and then prepare meals in our own kitchens. We prefer stopping into restaurants to grab a bite. Getting a stack of diner pancakes after a morning sono. Calling in a pizza after a retrieval. It's a perfect excuse to stay out of the kitchen! Unfortunately, all this eating out eats away at our funds.

And then the phone bill suddenly shoots through the roof. You're talking to friends and family (but only the ones who *don't* ask insensitive questions) longer and more frequently and not just on five-cent-a-minute Sundays.

Plus you're spending money on all sorts of reading materials. (Good thing this book was such a bargain!)

But not to worry. Whatever amount you invest will be well worth the years of joy the future holds. Plus, think of the guilt trip you'll be able to lay on your child years from now.

Say "Bye-bye" Sex Life

Remember when the two of you used to make love? Aaah, the good old days.

He'd give you that look, you'd reciprocate with a raised eyebrow and the kissing would begin. Long, hot passionate kisses that sent chills down your spine.

Then the clothes would fly. Tops, bottoms and everything in between. If you were too worked up to make it to the bedroom, you just did it there on the dining room table. Sounds like your former sex life? Even if it doesn't, it's probably what you fantasized about. Now, with the baby-making challenge consuming your every thought, your every ounce of energy, you don't even have the gumption to *think* this wild.

Lovemaking is now babymaking. Your head (and every other body part) went into a totally different zone the day "love" and "baby" traded places. The passion fizzles and the desire dims—for sex, that is. Now you're all hot and bothered by your baby-making endeavors.

If you're one of those couples whose treatment requires that they still do "it," hoping to time ovulation right, your sex life is probably quite methodical. Nothing takes the spontaneity out of lovemaking more than knowing you have to do the nasty between 1 and 3 in the afternoon. Hey, but at least you're still doing it.

However, if you're partaking of any form of ART, where it isn't necessary to be copulating at any specific time, or at all for that matter, then your sex life is probably on hold. A big hold. After hormone shots, blood testing and a sono—and I'm talking before breakfast—who wants to make love in the afternoon.

You're too afraid of hurting yourself and your organs and screwing up any possible chance of succeeding. And if you're awaiting a pregnancy test you're petrified that orgasm will cause a miscarriage. (But what if you fake orgasm? Does it still put you at risk?) Even more than any of these issues, you're just not in the mood.

Sure, you like to kiss and cuddle each other and share all kinds of affection. If your baby-making challenge doesn't tear the two of you apart it's sure to strengthen your love like nothing else can. But actual lovemaking? That's a different story. You have to get naked. And the most naked you've been lately is for your bootie shots, sonograms and morning shower.

Perhaps I'm representing a female mindset (or maybe just my own), but I know from my own husband that he was really turned off during our IVF cycle. All the things we used to do that pleasured ourselves physically suddenly were linked to a medical, scientific and clinical means of producing a child. Like standing naked in front of him. In the old days that could get things started, but, when engrossed in our IVF cycle, a bare bottom meant medication time.

We were too busy to care about orgasm. Fortunately, with hubby's frequent semen samples, he was still getting the release he claims most men can't live without. (Guys, is it true?)

And from what I hear, sex may never be what it once was. Many of my pregnant friends said they didn't have sex until AFTER the baby was born. Something about the husband being afraid that he'd bonk the little fetus' head with his pole of a penis. Maybe some of you guys are packing a wallop, but come on—you don't really believe this one? When these friends were finally doing it, they were merely squeezing it in while the baby was napping.

Anyway, sex—or should I say lovemaking—is overrated when you're baby-making challenged. (I'm trying to convince myself, OK?) At this point we'd rather focus our energies on baby-making. Besides, we have plenty of years to reacquaint ourselves once the baby is born. Come to think of it though, those pregnant friends said the sex thing never returned to normal even AFTER the baby arrived. So maybe I'm looking at a normal sex life again somewhere around the age of fifty.

Hey, but if you've been able to maintain that rare balance of lovemaking and babymaking, then more power to you. Many of us envy your position, whichever one it is that you two wild kids are into.

Say "Bye-bye" Caffeine and Other Goodies

Ice-cold iced tea. Hazelnut coffee, freshly brewed. Chocolate kisses, chocolate truffles, chocolate cookies and, of course, chocolate milk. What do all of these dietary staples have in common? The dreaded enemy, caffeine.

But is caffeine truly your enemy? There's all kinds of research out there that says it is but, there's also plenty of data that says, if consumed in moderation, caffeine is harmless.

Caffeine is a drug and aren't you taking enough of those at this point in your baby-making process? Some fertility doctors will insist that you cut out your morning jolt, while others will not even talk about it. My thought is that you want everything to be perfect right now—from being as well-rested as you can to cutting back on foods that *may* be harmful. You have nothing to lose.

Therefore, if you haven't kicked the habit already, do it now. (I mean *now*. Put a bookmark at this page, go to your refrigerator and toss all those nasty items right into the garbage.)

Yes, you love the zing you get from a morning cup of brew. I admit it—I was hooked, too. For days after I kicked the habit I was so lethargic and headachy I wanted to shoot myself. But I knew I had to sacrifice. Give up this one little nemesis in order to prepare a healthy environment for my baby. In no time you won't even miss it. Really. (I'm lying. Lying is a side effect of caffeine deprivation.)

As you subtract caffeinated goodies from your diet, don't forget to say bye-bye to other "treats"—alcohol, sushi, artificially sweetened crap that we still consume despite those poor laboratory rats, the cigar you've been smoking late at night, the glue you've been sniffing for kicks. Stuff like that.

There are some foods that are not quite as baby-making friendly as others. Consult your doctor on what these may be and start eliminating them from your diet immediately. Your baby will thank you.

While you're subtracting from your diet, don't forget about doing your addition—lots of water, fresh fruits and vegetables, and a nice blend of carbohydrates and protein. Eat like you're pregnant already. Your baby will thank you.

If an important guest were coming to stay in your home, wouldn't you change the sheets before she arrived? Wouldn't you clean the place up in order to make a good impression? If you'd make that kind of effort for some friend or relative for a weekend, why not prepare the "house," your body, for your future baby? Start cleaning up your diet now, hide away the coffee cups and prepare your "home" for the most precious guest you will ever have.

Forming Your
Own Play Group

As I partook in my IVF cycle, hubby encouraged me to sign up for a stress-management class sponsored by the hospital.

It was appropriately called the "Mind, Body" class, since my mind was racing with fear and my body, without my usual grueling daily exercise, was going to pot. Eight weeks of relaxation techniques, including yoga, mindful meditation and communication exercises, would do me good.

There we were, six baby-making challenged women in our thirties, sitting in the waiting room we all associated with, well, waiting. During the day we sat there waiting for blood tests but every Thursday night this room transformed into a relaxation sanctuary. Led by a non-baby-making challenged woman in her thirties, we went around the room explaining why we were here and what we hoped to get out of the class.

We were an eclectic group—three of us totally new to IVF, one of us on her second IVF cycle (the first miscarried), another who had already adopted a little girl and decided to give IVF one last try and, finally, one who was struggling with a secondary unexplained baby-making challenge. As we shared our fears and our desires to control them, we immediately felt connected. Like a group of substance abusers trying to kick their habit. A tribe of earth-conscious neighbors determined to clean up their town. A pow-wow of women chocoholics. A pack of tough high school girls hanging out in the bathroom.

We all dropped to the floor and began experimenting with yoga. Although we were supposed to keep our eyes closed to deepen the relaxation, many of us caught each other peeking between downward dog and warrior poses.

As the weeks rolled by and we continued to breathe deeply, lengthening each yoga pose, we got to know one another. We became a tight clan, a group, a gang.

After class we'd hang out in the parking lot talking (not smoking) until way past 10 p.m. We'd make jokes in class and heckled the instructor the day she brought us each an orange and taught us how to "be at one with our fruit." (Yet another orange encounter!)

Like a bunch of schoolgirls, we tried our best to pay attention—slowly breaking open the rind and focusing our senses on each section, the texture in our mouths, the scent on our fingers, the mess on the floor. We couldn't help but giggle in between bites.

All we needed to make our gang more official was pink satin jackets with "Mommas in the Makin'" written across the back in black scripty lettering. Even after we graduated from class, tons more relaxed than when we first started, the gang stayed together. Through retrievals and transfers, shots and emotional swings, we've been there for one another, checking in while dining out or talking on the phone. And we're all working on forming a future gang—our children's play group!

After all, gang members have always looked out for one another. *West Side Story*'s Sharks and Jets. The Pink Ladies from the movie *Grease*. These gang members stuck together through thick and thin. We "Mommas in the Makin'" were just as passionate about our group; the only difference was we didn't carry knives—we carried needles.

If you're looking for a way to alleviate your stress, check around for gang-forming opportunities . . . classes, support groups, a friend of a friend, whatever. And forget about being indoctrinated—your baby-making challenge and a willingness to share your feelings with others should be your automatic in.

Do the Hokey-
Needle-Pokey

You may have figured this out by now, but I've been afraid of needles my entire life. The thought of being injected with a hormone-suppressing drug every day was putting me on the verge of yet another faint.

Any shot I've ever experienced has always been in the arm. Not in the butt, leg or stomach. Isn't that where they get the expression "a shot in the arm"? Not a shot in the gut.

There are many types of medications designed to suppress ovulation. Each one works by quieting the ovaries (and Lord knows mine are just too noisy) before you embark on a stimulation phase.

My shot was to be administered an inch or so below my belly button every night before dinner. Like many other women faced with this chore, I had my husband do it for me. The needle was scary enough. The needle in my own hand was downright terrifying.

I remember the very first night. We both stood nervously around the kitchen counter spreading out the items necessary for this science experiment: a tiny vial of medication, 27-gauge needles (the higher the number, the thinner the needle. If you ever inadvertently get 7-gauge needles you might experience some pain—the needle would be about the circumference of a drain pipe!), alcohol wipes to clean the counter top and my stomach. (Now really, how dirty could my stomach be? First thing every morning I shower. I put on a fresh pair of underwear and a pair of slacks. I don't usually undo my pants during lunch so there is no chance of sauce splattering down there. I could see if we had to inject the needle inside my bellybutton, then perhaps we'd have a cleanliness issue. That bellybutton smell, a few tiny particles of fuzz—now those are health hazards.)

We wiped my skin clean. As the alcohol dried on my skin, hubby drew back the units of cold clear fluid. (We were instructed to store the medicine in the fridge. My biggest fear was that it would freeze up so I kept raising the thermostat until my water bottles were beading with sweat and my cream cheese melted down to mush.)

He handed the needle off to me. I was the official bubble checker. When you're getting an injection, you want to be sure there are no large bubbles in the syringe or you'll be injecting air into your body. (And most of us are already full of hot air.)

A few flicks of my fingers against the top of the syringe easily popped out any unwanted air. Then I handed the needle back to him.

Assume position. Sit on edge of kitchen chair, pants open around my hips like some guy who just gorged himself on beer and pasta, pinch an inch of flesh (or as much as you have to offer) and close your eyes. He got down on his knees to be eye level with my navel and poked in the appropriate spot. A few more wipes with the alcohol swab and the ritual was complete. Total time, from prep to poke: approximately eight minutes.

Like anything in life, you get better with practice. We went through two fourteen-day kits—about a month's worth of hormone-suppressing shots. How suppressing.

Those hormone-suppressing kits, complete with all the goodies necessary for shot administration, reminded me of cosmetic counter packages you get free with purchase. You know, the ones with the lipstick, nail polish and eyeliner, all wrapped up in a dainty little box. Everything a girl needs to feel pretty.

Some hormone suppressing kits are packaged in a similar tiny box, closed tight with a wafer seal. Upon cracking open the seal, you'll find the tiny vial of medicine, securely wrapped syringes, a handful of alcohol swabs and, of course, an information sheet. Everything a girl needs to feel pretty nervous about the IVF process.

The shots continued and, on many days, I thought I would never survive this process. Subcutaneous shots in the stomach aren't all that painful—but you have to do them everyday at pretty much the same time. I was always thinking about the shot I just got and the one I would get next. My days, and my mind, were consumed by injection therapy.

Then, one day hubby was out of town on business and I was on my own. The anxiety was building in my pincushion stomach. *You can do this. You can do this.* I psyched myself up as I sat on the edge of the chair and prepared my shot.

Measuring and eyeing, leveling and spritzing, I felt like a cross between a heroin addict and a physician. I looked at the thin little tip. *C'mon, this is no big deal,* I tried to convince myself. I knew it wouldn't hurt but the act of shooting, rather than the shot itself, was making me sick.

Do it fast, like hari-kari. I wanted to close my eyes but that wouldn't have made sense. Quickly I jabbed the point into a fleshy part of meat and pressed down fast, releasing the hormonal stream into my system. Needle out. A spot of blood so small you'd think I pricked myself sewing was whisked away by a sterile swab. I did it!

This was a milestone. I was so proud, I wanted to do it again. When my husband returned from his meeting the next day, he began to prepare my shot. "I got it, hon." A new woman was born.

Not that I gave up my fear of needles. One successful morning is not going to take away a lifetime of phobia. But it was a start. And a start would come in handy, especially with shots of a hormone stimulant starting in a matter of days.

I was so fixated on the act of giving and receiving my hormone-suppressing shots that I forgot to stop and notice how I was feeling physically. And then it dawned on me—I was feeling like a man. Void of any femininity. My breasts looked punier than usual. I was wearing a lot of sweatpants and sweatshirts. And I think I caught myself scratching one time.

I was menopausal, years before my time. Hot flashes, cold flashes, dry mouth, dry you know what, a smidge moody. My ovaries just shut down, like an ovarian blackout. An ovarian strike. No one was producing. No one was working the way they're supposed to. Both the left and the right were slacking off. I could feel the inactivity.

But not for long.

A Hormonal Swing Set

How I feared getting the hormone stimulation shots. Everyone told me I'd turn into a homicidal maniac, that my moods would swing higher than a trapeze artist. That I'd get bloated and fat (which would give me even more reason to be super bitchy).

Before any of my hormone shots, when I was still a rational and sane woman, I imagined myself transforming from Dr. Jekyl to Mr. Hyde. Turning into a wild beast, an animal. One moment I'd be thinking clearly as Dr. Jekyl himself, but as the night closes in I'd become a hormonally crazed monster. Crying over bad movies, yelling about the toilet seat being up, throwing a hissy fit if I burned dinner. Hair lying wildly upon my head, knuckles dragging on the floor. And my first victim? Who else but spouse.

Of course you won't mean anything you say or do, which is why I suggest you apologize now before you even begin hormone stimulation. Tell him and the others you love that you don't know what kind of a maniac you will turn into and whatever you do or say, you're sorry.

Tell them now before it's too late!

Then again, you may not feel the least bit moody from your hormones. You may not feel a thing.

To my surprise, I wasn't too bitchy. In fact, I was quite pleasant and so relieved. However, since I had already given the Jekyl/Hyde speech to my loved ones, they were prepared for the worst so, anytime I said the slightest off-color comment, they immediately reminded me, "Take it easy. You're not yourself, remember?"

I could feel my ovaries growing at a rapid pace inside my abdomen. Percolating, bubbling over, gurgle, gurgle. Talk about a weird feeling. And the longer I took the shots, the more my ovaries were producing extra follicles that kept growing in size. After about five days of stimulation I felt as if I had gorged myself at an all-you-can-eat buffet. Unfortunately, the food missed my stomach and dropped right into my pelvic cavity. All of it just sitting there, feeling as if it would burst out of my skin.

In the stimulation phase the doctors keep a close eye on you. Blood work and sonos quite often, sometimes every day. Watching, measuring and waiting to see how much your body responds. During my first sono, which was three days after beginning my stimulation hormone, I had produced around a half dozen follicles ranging in size. By the last sono, which was nine days after beginning hormones, I had more than doubled my output! I was busting—literally.

Hubby and I felt so proud. My ovaries had done good. What a pair they are. In no time I would be ready for my hCG shot.

Foods You Probably <u>Won't</u> Be Craving During Your Stimulation

eggs Benedict

egg foo young

eggnog

eggs over easy

scrambled eggs

egg noodles

egg drop soup

egg bagels

egg salad

deviled eggs

hard-boiled eggs

eggs

Add your own non-craved foods here so that your spouse knows never to offer them to you:

_____

_____

_____

_____

What to Read When You're Really Hormonal

this book

stupid supermarket tabloids

comic books

old love letters

the funnies

Add your own choices here
to serve as a reminder list:

_____

_____

_____

_____

What <u>Not</u> to Read When You're Really Hormonal

Rosemary's Baby

Frankenstein

Sleeping With the Enemy

How to Murder Your Husband

I Married An Axe Murderer

One Flew Over the Cuckoo's Nest

warning labels

instruction booklets for electronic goods

Add your own titles here to serve as a reminder list:

_____

_____

_____

_____

Growing Pains

Every month the female body is supposed to produce one egg. One measly little egg. You know how crampy you can feel when that happens. Now, imagine that your body produced anywhere between 8 and 50 eggs that same month. You're bound to feel awful!

When we women are hormone induced and full of mega cartons of eggs, we tend to walk a little funny. If you haven't experienced the walk yet yourself, here's how to identify it:

She's the girl hanging out in the waiting room at the doctor's office. While everyone else is either stone-faced or making silly grins, she has a look of discomfort. Not a pain look but more like a "I just smelled something bad" look.

She might be sitting sideways with her knees hugged up toward her chest. This has been known to relieve some of the pressure in the abdomen. Her hand may be resting on her forehead and if she were to speak she'd probably say, "Nurse, call my f—kin' name already!"

And when they do finally call her name, you'll notice her slow rise out of the chair. Never standing fully erect, she begins the walk. A slow shuffle, body slightly bent forward, head hanging down as if she were looking for loose change on the carpet. The arms swing ever so slightly so as not to cause any quick movements that will make her fullness feel even stranger than it already does. If Mr. Significant Other is at her side, he usually has one arm around her back, one hand nervously stuffed in his pocket and a brow knitted as tightly as a sweater.

Women who walk like this may be nearing the end of a cycle and are on the verge of getting their hCG shot. Or they're doing one heck of a Charlie Chaplin impression.

Now I Know My hCGs

They say in life everyone gets 15 minutes of fame. Plus, there's the window of opportunity we're always searching for.

Here's a riddle: what do you get when you cross your 15 minutes of fame with your window of opportunity? Your hCG shot!

Human chorionic gonadotropin (hCG—not HSG, that's your ping thing) is normally produced by the developing embryo when it implants into the uterine lining. Its main action is hang around until the placenta has developed enough to take over the production of hormones. But when you're engaged in an IVF cycle, hCG is administered artificially in an IM (intramuscular, which means the rump, remember!) shot. Its main purpose is to help time ovulation so that the follicles can be harvested properly.

When you're participating in a form of ART, hCG is typically given when the stimulation phase is complete. The hCG tricks the body into thinking it's ovulating, tricks the couple into thinking they are not going to survive the administration of this pivotal shot, thus releasing the follicles from the ovaries. Some say the hCG helps to loosen the follicles. I, for one, think nerves finally pop 'em out.

So why is the "h" lower case and the "CG" always capitalized? Is the human part less significant than the chorionic gonadotropin part? I think it should read Hcg, with the emphasis on human, mankind, life. It would be the respectable thing to do, considering all that we're going through. Thank you for agreeing.

When the stimulation phase is complete, all blood levels are where they should be and your sono shows the right picture, the medical team will let you know when your 15-minute window of fame and opportunity will occur.

123

For us, it was a Tuesday night before bed, 11:30 p.m. That meant the shot could be administered no more than 15 minutes later. Such pressure. So many things to prepare. So many people to inform. And I had never done this before. Couldn't we have a dress rehearsal?

Welcome back, my dear friend the orange. Practice darting the needle in, said the nurse—not jabbing and definitely not poking—just darting. You mean to tell me that the average person can distinguish between a jab, a poke and a dart? C'mon. We need to use more extreme words—plunge, stab, ram, beat, pound, obliterate, maul, mangle. Then maybe we'll be able to differentiate.

The night of the event, hubby ran to the nearest grocer and came back with one orange, one grapefruit. I pictured him in the produce section, contemplating whether his wife's butt cheek looked more like sweet juicy fruit or the one that leaves your lips permanently puckered together. The way my backside was looking those days, with mega-hormones and minimal exercise, he could have rightfully brought back a watermelon.

We were relieved to be given a time prior to our normal bedtime. The thought of falling asleep while waiting to give a shot in the middle of the night was nerve-wracking. Fifteen minutes prior to our big moment we began setting up.

Sterilize the counter top. Draw back the needle. Mix the ampule of powder with the saline solution. Flick the bubbles. Drop pants around ankles. (I went from having my pants hang around my hips for the earlier hormone shots to around my ankles with hCG. At this rate, I'd be naked by progesterone.) Wipe down my rump with alcohol. Bend over. Relax knee on the side the shot was going in. This kept the butt muscle from tensing up. Breathe. hCG shot complete. And we still had a full five minutes left to bask in our 15 minute window of fame and opportunity.

Or to pass out.

A Lesson In
Giving and Retrieving

In the old days, prior to our baby-making challenge, the word "retrieval" conjured up thoughts of a beautiful Yellow Labrador running after a wooden stick on a lovely spring afternoon.

Or perhaps you've heard the term "harvesting." Just picture it—a sweet little girl skipping through the apple orchards, holding a delicate straw basket, plucking macintosh, granny smith and golden delicious from the trees up above.

To a couple going through IVF, retrieval and harvesting mean much more. It's the day the doctor dives in, does his deep-sea fishing and gathers up all the follicular gems he can find in a woman's uterine cavity.

My abdomen was about to burst with eggs. I was so uncomfortable. None of my zippered pants fit, I could barely wear a seatbelt and I even found it hard to wear certain underwear. (If they weren't oversized, granny panties, I felt quite irritated.) I couldn't wait to have that flat feeling again. But the fear of the retrieval was making me feel ill in another sense. Would the eggs be of good quality? The moment of truth was approaching.

The morning of retrieval I had to remind myself *not* to do the normal things I always do. Yes, I could pee but I couldn't drink. No water, juice or scotch on the rocks.

Then I hopped in the shower but couldn't put on moisturizing lotion afterwards. No deodorant. No mascara or lipstick. No gentle spritz of perfume. I'd be going in to the sterile operating room void of the things that make a girl feel girlie.

Hubby was expected to produce a semen sample around 9:00 a.m. and I was scheduled for pre-ops at 9:30. The night before, neither of us had admitted our greatest fear. What if he had a wet dream? His semen had to store up for three to five days. A wet dream would have been devastating to the process we had already invested months into. Years, if you count the original day we finally said "OK, let's make a baby."

The night before I purposely dressed in my most unattractive pajamas. We watched lots of news and cooking shows on TV. And our kiss good-night was rather blah. Fortunately, he didn't dream of sex.

The next morning we went to the hospital, where he produced his sample in less than 15 minutes. There must have been lots of fresh dirty magazines, great porno movies or a hooker in the room. Whatever the case, he had completed his part the best he could. What a load off his, uh, mind. Now it was my turn.

I changed into a sterile outfit. Blue gown with ties in the back (I could feel the air blowing on my bare bottom), cafeteria worker's hair net (I had a strong desire to serve mashed potatoes to a long line of kids) and non-slip booties on my feet (which I stole after the procedure. But is that stealing? They couldn't use them again therefore, they were garbage).

The nurse took my vitals. Heart rate nervously beating above normal. Temperature OK. The standard interview: name, date of birth, social security number, allergies, experiences with anesthesia. I passed the test. We were ready to proceed.

I was escorted into the operating room by a nurse who happened to be wearing the exact same outfit as me. And there was my doctor—looking like a god—cloaked in a sterile gown, wearing a mask across his face. He was a vision of loveliness. I felt my knees weaken. After helping me up on the table, the anesthesiologist hooked his sleep serum into my arm and in no time I was out.

Even though I was out for the entire process, I had visualized the scene dozens of times prior to this big day. I had imagined myself, legs akimbo, as the doctor took his suction device and sucked the eggs out of me, one by one. As if he were harvesting apples, I pictured him placing each egg into a little basket which he held in the crook of his arm. La, la, la, he hummed.

I had been warned that you can lose all self-control under anesthesia and do really embarrassing things, like break wind. What if

I passed gas right there in the doctor's face while he was merrily harvesting? I wouldn't know nor could I apologize or try to blame it on the anesthesiologist.

Outside, on the other side of the infamous door that separated the cruel world from this sterile, magical world, sat hubby, waiting like an expectant father on the day of delivery. Finally, the doctor came out with news: "You had sixteen eggs. She's fine. We're off to a good start." Hubby was a proud papa. Pass out the cigars.

Blink, blink and I was awake. Lying on a stretcher in the recovery room. I felt a little crampy and a teeny bit groggy, as if I had just awakened from a short nap. Hubby came in and sat behind the curtain with me for an hour or two before we were released to go home. There were lots of other little curtains drawn in the same area, like the dressing room at Loehmann's. How many of us were in there behind closed sheets? And somewhere in that very same building was another room where all our many eggs sat waiting for something magical to happen.

QUIZ #3:

If Over a Dozen Eggs Are Retrieved, a Butch Mature and a Few Fertilize, How Fast is the Bus Going?

The Pitter-Patter of Fertilization Results

How fast *is* the bus going? It's like those crazy math questions you got on your SAT exams. The ones where you thought it was impossible to know the answer. Well, waiting for your fertilization results after retrieval is as much of a mystery.

The doctor had retrieved sixteen eggs from me, twelve had matured (which meant they survived and were of large enough size) and eight had been fertilized, but we had no clue how many would survive for transfer.

A day truly can make a difference. And two days can determine whether or not you'll progress to the transfer stage. In the past, embryos were transferred into a woman's uterus three days after retrieval. But in a relatively new study, one which we signed up for and were accepted, our embryos were transferred on day five.

It's called Blast. And the studies support waiting until day five—the blastocyte stage—to see which embryos are developing well and which are not. Fewer embryos are implanted, thereby reducing the chance for multiples. Blast may be the technical term for this procedure but it's also a good choice of word for the experience. The day you receive positive fertilization results is most definitely a blast.

Do Not Go Boom After an IM Shot

The night after retrieval begins a new phase in your IVF cycle: progesterone shots. We were instructed to administer this IM (intramuscular) shot in the PM (post meridian), so we chose right before sleep. This way I didn't have to sit up on a sore rump.

If you had a "natural" pregnancy, your body would automatically begin to produce greater amounts of progesterone. This would help your uterine lining to thicken and prepare for the embryo nuzzling in for the winter. With IVF, progesterone shots simulate what nature intended the body to do.

For a while you'll think YM (why me?). You might even start reading YM (*Young Miss*) to recapture your youth and distract you from these very adult issues. You'll have pain every time you sit down to make a BM (bowel movement). And when you awake in the AM (ante meridian), you'll feel your butt cheeks stiff and sore. All because of this IM injection.

To make giving the shot simpler for your spouse (and hopefully, he is able to do it for this is a real tricky one to do yourself), you may want to ask the nurse to mark your butt with a pen. "X" marks the spot. Actually it was an "O," a circle, marking off the circumference of the areas on each cheek. Tic, tac, toe, anyone?

For weeks I kept retracing these two circles on the upper outer quadrants of both buttock cheeks. At first, we used a simple Bic pen but the ink kept washing away in the shower. So, we graduated to a thick black marker. If it were up to my nervous hubby, we would have moved on to spray paint. Fortunately, the marker did the trick. In time, my rear end looked like a face with two black circles for eyes, both bloodshot with red needle pricks.

133

As the weeks roll by and your bottom grows black and blue and scabby, remember that you may remain on progesterone for the first few weeks of your pregnancy. So, even though this may be a miserable and painful experience, not having the shots would feel much worse.

Your Pride and Joy:
the Transfer

For me, the transfer was the most emotional moment in my entire IVF cycle.

It was the day I saw life . . . the day life was placed inside of me . . . the day I went home pregnant.

I put on the same cute sterile outfit I wore in retrieval. (It was a fresh version.) They even gave me a new pair of non-skid booties (which I stole again) and I lay on the same operating table in the same operating room. It felt like *déjà vu* all over again. But this time I was totally awake, prepared to experience the insemination process of my future children.

High up on the wall was a TV screen that was really nothing more than a highly-magnified picture of my embryos. There they were, two round dots, one atop the other. My babies! So what if they looked like the two circles on my butt at that very moment. They were mine, ours. Talk about live TV! I felt the urge to wave at them and tell them both that Mommy loved them.

After confirming my name, date of birth and all other particulars that ensured the embryos were ours, the embryologist, who was in an adjacent room with a large glass window, gently sucked the two little bubbles into a catheter. Mind you, everything I was seeing was magnified thousands of times on this high-tech TV screen.

Then the embryologist walked through the door, separating her room of life with my sterile environment, and handed the catheter off to the doctor. They both handled my babies so gingerly. Despite the cool room and my lack of clothing, I felt warm all over. The doctor inserted the catheter into my vagina and proceeded to position the embryos into my uterus. His every move

135

was clearly documented on a tiny screen that he watched with great concentration. At the same time, I was watching a different TV screen, the one hooked up to the ultrasound pressing on my belly. All the preceding months of torture and pain were a blur at the moment. I never felt happier.

Home sweet home, I heard someone say as the embryos were tucked neatly into place. I could feel the tears flowing down my temples as I lay still. A nurse from behind my head handed me a tissue. I couldn't see her but I understood why she was there.

As I was rolled out of the operating room, I was handed a black-and-white photograph of our embryos in their petri dish. For the next 30 minutes I lay motionless in the recovery room while my loving husband held my hand and stared at the picture of our two beautiful embryos. We looked at the photo lovingly as if the two tiny "babies" inside of me at the very moment had names, faces and little personalities.

Even if just for those few fleeting moments, we were pregnant.

Family Photos

By the time you reach the transfer phase you will feel as if you already have children. Even if they are just a few days old, your embryos are real and very much alive. But the clincher—the thing that really made our embryos feel like babies—was the picture we went home with the day of transfer.

It felt like a cross between a birth certificate and a first photo session at Sears. There they were, two gorgeous circles, each centered in its own little picture frame. With just our name and date of transfer to identify them, this picture represented a priceless Kodak moment.

To us, those two simple circles were like little pictures of bald-headed babies with adorable smiles. Very real, very much ours and we get to take them home today!

You'll find yourself clinging to this photo as if it's a picture of the most precious little cutie(s) in the world. (Probably because, to you both, it is.) For the first time ever, our babies were more than just pictures in our minds. They were black-and-white stills taken straight from the petri dish.

Staring deeply into these little cherubic faces, I see the best of both of us. One circle, all neat and perfect, is my baby girl. An angel (like her Mom, no doubt). The other circle, a larger and sloppier version, a bit fragmented and disheveled, is more like dear old Dad after a rough-and-tumble kind of day.

I imagine showing these pictures to my children one day and saying "Look how cute you guys were." But until that day arrives, you too will find yourself clinging to these pictures because in our situation they truly are worth a thousand words.

Bundle Up—it's Chilly
in There

I was about to cryo. Two little embryos were hopefully nuzzling into my warm and fully lined uterus. But just in case our "IVFforts" did not work this time, we signed up for embryo freezing, also known as cryopreservation.

Embryos have to qualify for this amazing technique. They must look strong, healthy and zesty enough to survive not just the freeze itself, but the thaw.

Cryopreservation, along with all the other parts of IVF, is a spectacular breakthrough in medical science. It's like putting a fur coat in cold storage for the summer. Or freezing meat in the basement cooler because you got such a great discount at the market and who needs to go shopping again after you already went through the exhausting effort.

If we were to use cryo for the embryos that hadn't been implanted in me, all I could picture was my poor little babies shivering in a big cold cooler. No coats or blankets. Just their naked little bodies all frosty and chilled, like cubes in a freezer.

Having embryos in cold storage for a limited time allows couples to undergo a cycle without going through the emotionally wrecking suppression/ stimulation cycle as well as the retrieval. There have even been cases of successful pregnancies years after the initial freeze. It's a wonderful option for some.

Unfortunately, our remaining embryos didn't qualify for cryo. The embryology team determined that they weren't strong enough to survive the thaw. We were disappointed, for it felt like we had lost a bunch of our children. Yet, we were glad that the decision for future babies had been taken out of our hands. There were so many of them. At least we didn't have to worry now if we would eventually go back to attempt to make babies with every one.

For now, we would focus our energy on the two survivors who were hopefully growing strong inside of me.

SECTION VI: FINAL STEPS

The Pregnancy Results

Yummy, Yummy, Yummy, Please Let Me Have Baby in the Tummy

You're winding down. Fewer shots, fewer visits to the doctor's office. You're now in the waiting period. Only a few thousand days until Christmas and a little more than a week until your pregnancy test.

Your best bet is to keep busy and not let your thoughts run away with you because they will. Thoughts are very good runners and they have been practicing some major sprints throughout your baby-making challenge. Your thoughts are in superb condition, pumped and buff, ready to run away with you if you let them.

Instead, relax as much as possible. Avoid stressful situations. Cuddle with each another. And remember to keep marking your rump for those all-important progesterone shots.

Feeling pregnant is not important at this point. Many women have felt nauseous, bloated and tired and were not pregnant—they were just nervous. Conversely, many women have felt completely unchanged and were pregnant. Stop trying to figure it out. Rent lots of movies. Read books. Stay occupied.

The day of the pregnancy test will be here soon enough. OK, maybe not soon enough but eventually. Yes, I know the time suddenly turns into dog years, lingering on and on until you're ready to drop. But your day will come. Not before you know it but when it is scheduled to happen.

You've gotten this far—hang in there.

Funny Movies to Watch While Waiting for Your Pregnancy Test

American Pie

Parenthood

Naked Gun

Airplane

Police Academy

Junior

Grease

When Harry Met Sally

Three Men and A Baby

The Nutty Professor

Look Who's Talking

Mrs. Doubtfire

your wedding video

an exercise video from the 1980s

Add your own titles here to serve as a rental reminder list:

_____

_____

_____

_____

Movies <u>Not</u> to Watch if You're Worried About Multiples

101 Dalmatians

Cheaper by the Dozen

Ten

9 1/2 Weeks

Eight Men Out

Snow White and the 7 Dwarves

6 Degrees of Separation

Rocky V, IV, III and II

Multiplicity

Twins

any other movie with a large number in the title

Add your own titles here to serve as a non-rental reminder list:

_____

_____

_____

_____

Foods to Eat While Waiting for Your Pregnancy Test (To Help You Think Baby)

animal crackers

peanut butter and jelly sandwiches

ice cream

cookies and milk

bananas

Cheerios

chicken fingers

any form of finger food

mushy things

baby artichokes

baby carrots

items from the children's menu

Add your own foods here, those that make you think baby:

_____

_____

_____

_____

Toys to Distract You While Waiting for Your Pregnancy Test

computers

the Internet

board games

beauty salons

spas (just no saunas!)

long drives

card games

shopping malls

food

the phone

slow, easy walks

gossip

Add your own things here to serve as a distraction list:

_____

_____

_____

_____

One-liners to Tell People Who Can't Stop Asking if You're Pregnant

We won't know for at least a few months.

We won't know for at least a few years.

I really can't talk about it now.

Thank you for understanding if I don't answer that question.

Please don't ask us anymore. We'll tell
you when there's news to share.

Everytime you ask that question, you jinx us. Do you
want to be responsible for any bad news?

I'm afraid to talk about it so let's not.

I can't talk about it so let's not.

It's a secret.

It's highly confidential information.

Rome wasn't built in a day.

I can't stand the heat so you better get out of my kitchen.

[Spouse's first name] has forbidden me to talk about it.

Let's change the subject.

No offense but it's none of your beeswax.

We'll discuss this later. And next time wait for me to bring it up.

Sorry, but I'm having trouble hearing you.

Things to Reflect on While Waiting for Your Pregnancy Test

Rather than offer you a list of the many things you can reflect on while waiting for the day of your pregnancy test, I thought this would be an opportune time to think about a group of people who have gotten you this far. Above and beyond your spouse, your friends and your family, let's give a moment of thoughtfulness to your medical team.

You know how everyone always talks about doctors as gods? Well, in our case you can understand why.

They are the gods and goddesses of baby-making challenged couples. Their work, their discoveries, their dedication give us a good chance of conceiving when at one point in our lives our chances seemed pretty slim. Maybe it's taken you a few months, perhaps a few years for you to get to this pivotal point in your baby-making process. Your medical team played a huge role in helping you arrive.

Bless those doctors who have a sense of humor and a bedside manner that helps them maintain their humanity. Bless them all for sweating it out in med school. This is one time we won't dare complain about their fees.

Thank heavens for the nurses who keep their cool, level heads despite the insanity that we're involved in. Their frequent contact with us is priceless.

Praise the staff at the front desk who greet you with a smile each morning, remember your name and maintain a sense of professionalism in all situations.

Hallelujah for the embryologists who work diligently behind the scenes, uniting eggs and sperm into happy, magical embryos.

And kudos to the phlebotomists who draw countless tubes of blood each day. Thanks for keeping squeamish women like me from passing out.

By now, you're probably so attached to your medical team that you never, ever want to leave them. Even after you get pregnant, even after you have the baby, even after the kid goes off to college—you'll still want to visit with the team who helped you conquer your baby-making challenge.

So as you wait for the day of your pregnancy test, remember that, no matter what results come in, a miracle has already occurred.

The Baby Announcement

Here we are nearing the end of the baby-making challenge. At first I had written a few chapters on all the different ways your challenge could turn out—baby, no baby, I need a break from all of this, baby. But then I remembered what I had told you pages and pages ago—that this book isn't about the end result, it's about the process you're taking to get to it.

Therefore, I am not going to explore the "results." Instead, I am inviting you to explore yours with me once they happen.

Email me at *bmchumor@aol.com*
("bmchumor" stands for baby-making challenged humor!)

Until then, dear fellow baby-making challenged couple, hang in there, keep your love strong and laugh whenever you can. You will survive!

SECTION VII: THE A,B,Cs

A HA!ndy Glossary of Common Terms and Procedures

On the following pages you will find familiar baby-making challenged terms and procedures with unfamiliar **HA!** (**H**umorous **A**ngle) definitions. Have fun!

AI (artificial insemination)
HA! a procedure where a technician or physician uses a turkey baster to squirt sperm into a woman at the time of ovulation.

ART (assisted reproductive technology)
HA! a cool term you can use later on when describing your baby: "She is a work of ART!"

BBT (basal body temperature)
HA! that first thing you may have to do each morning, before even getting out of bed, when really all you want to do is pee-pee.

Baby-making challenged
HA! the new term for infertility that will be used into the next millennium.

Cervical fluid
HA! the stuff your doctor asks you to look for each month; the stuff that reminds you of what you blow out your nose.

Cervix
HA! the one part of your body you've never felt but your doctor sure has—many, many times.

Condom
HA! something your mate uses less often than the probe at the doctor's office.

Donor insemination
HA! a no-backsies situation.

Embryo
HA! the most beautiful word you can hear other than "pregnant."

Embryologist
HA! the person you may never meet, the one you want to kiss from head to toe.

Fallopian tubes
HA! the reproductive pick-up joint; the place where sperm normally meets the egg for drinks and further intimacies!

Fertilization
HA! everything we've been talking about through this entire book!

GIFT (gamete intra fallopian transfer)
HA! something you no longer think of as an item received around the holidays, one you're apt to return.

hCG (human chorionic gonadotropin)
HA! your 15-minute window of fame and opportunity.

Hostile mucus
HA! that phlegm-ball your grandfather has been coughing up and choking down for the last 50 years.

IVF (in vitro fertilization)
HA! an expensive procedure that may cost more than your wedding!

Laparoscopy

HA! also known as a laptop-roscopy, an examination of the pelvic organs while holding a laptop computer.

MESA and TESA

HA! procedures that sound southwestern.

Morphology

HA! a rating that shows the shape of things to cum.

Motility

HA! a rating that shows whether or not sperm can swim like an Olympic champion or sink like bricks.

Oocyte

HA! originally known as an ocyte (one "o") but lots of grown-ups ooo-ed and ahhh-ed at these cute little ova, so the new phrase *oooocyte* stuck.

Ovary

HA! the hardest working organ in any ART cycle. What a pair!

Pap smear

HA! also referred to as pap schmear; goes well with bagels.

Progesterone

HA! the shot in the butt that makes it impossible for you to sit down.

Semen analysis

HA! an embarrassing moment when a guy carries his manhood around in a cup.

Superovulation
HA! a super-cool comic book character who can fight baby-making challenges in a single bound.

Varicocele
HA! varicose veins in the testicles which can be caused by poor circulation; if so, men are instructed to stop crossing their balls when they sit.

Zygote
HA! a rare animal at the petting zoo.

SECTION VIII: SITE-SEEING

Web Sites Worth Logging On To

To give you a jumpstart on the "homework" phase of your baby-making challenge, here's a brief list of Web sites you might want to check out.

AIA
The American Infertility Association
www.americaninfertility.org

RESOLVE
www.resolve.org

INCIID
(pronounced "inside")
The International Council On Infertility Information
and Dissemination, Inc.
www.inciid.org

ASRM
American Society for Reproductive Medicine
www.asrm.org

ICSI
International Consumer Support for Infertility
www.icsi.ws/

SSR
Society for the Study of Reproduction
www.ssr.org

National Center for Health Statistics
www.cdc.gov/nchswww

NetHealth Internet Guide
www.infertility.com

Lisa Safran

The End . . .
and, Hopefully,
the Beginning!